Mystic Places

Mystic Places

By the Editors of Time-Life Books

TIME-LIFE BOOKS, ALEXANDRIA, VIRGINIA

CONTENTS

Paradise Lost

Thousands of years after it supposedly sank into the cold and gloomy depths of the Atlantic Ocean, the island continent of Atlantis lives on as one of history's most tantalizing puzzles. If indeed such a place existed, Atlantis was a civilization unequaled before or since. Yet its chroniclers say that it vanished in little more than a single day, leaving not a trace behind.

The oldest and fullest surviving account of the great island's rise and fall was provided by the Greek philosopher Plato in the fourth century B.C. According to Plato's description — illustrated at left and on pages 15-17 — Atlantis was a land where skilled agriculturists created sweet-scented orchards and where animals, including "a very large stock of elephants," flourished. Within its chief city were innumerable mansions outdone in grandeur only by the royal palace and by the nearby temple raised to honor Poseidon. But neither gold nor glory could save the Atlanteans from themselves. Their growing materialism mightily offended the gods, wrote Plato, and the whole civilization was condemned to a swift and spectacular end.

Atlantis has often been linked with other places of mystery, among them the pyramids of Egypt and the stone slabs of Stonehenge. Unlike those brooding monuments, however, the land that Plato portrayed is no more tangible than memory or dreams. But many people believe that the drowned country's wealth of silver, copper, and gold still glimmers for the finding on the ocean floor. Perhaps one day, they say, some bold salvager may even bring to light Atlantis's fabled golden tablets, graven with the laws of earthly paradise.

Dressed for a balmy climate and surrounded by wild animals that have nothing to fear from humans, Atlanteans pursue a life of cultivated leisure amid the gardens of a great mansion.

A City of Surpassing Splendor

Chief among the many splendors of Plato's Atlantis was the sprawling palace compound. Built on a low hill in the center of the capital and ringed by three canals, the structures that made up the royal residence opened onto a courtyard containing the temple of Poseidon. The complex was erected by Atlas, eldest son of Poseidon and the first high king of Atlantis. But the sovereigns who succeeded Atlas on the throne were hardly content to leave this locus of their power as they found it. "As each king received it from his predecessor," Plato wrote, "he added to its adornment and did all he could to surpass the king before him, until finally they made of it an abode amazing to behold for the magnitude and beauty of its workmanship."

Visitors to the palace compound *(right)* entered along a broad concourse that crossed the three canals, passing through portals that breached a wall of brass, a wall of tin, and an innermost wall of copper that "sparkled like fire." Within the embrace of these gleaming barriers were residences of the aristocracy — mansions of white and black and red stone quarried from the native rock. Everywhere stood grandeur almost beyond the power of words to describe. "The wealth they possessed," wrote Plato of the Atlantean monarchs, "was so immense that the like had never been seen before in any royal house nor will ever easily be seen again."

Wisdom beyond Mortal Measure

The spiritual center of Atlantis was the temple of Poseidon, a magnificent building at the heart of the palace compound. Here, the continent's rulers met to hand down their laws.

The temple was dazzling testimony to the metalworking skills of the Atlanteans. Encircled with a wall of gold, the exterior of the building was, according to Plato, "coated with silver, save only the pinnacles, and these they coated with gold. As to the interior, they made the ceiling all of ivory . . . variegated with gold and silver and orichalcum [copper], and all the rest of the walls and pillars and floors they covered with orichalcum." An immense golden figure of Poseidon driving six winged steeds dominated the temple's central court; statues of sea nymphs gleamed from every shadowed crevice.

The high king of Atlantis and his nine brothers, princes of the nine other provinces, gathered every five or six years in this awe-inspiring forum (right). After sacrificing a bull and making it an offering to their gods, the dark-robed rulers gathered around the fading embers and passed judgments, inscribing them upon a golden tablet. Wisely governed, the people of Atlantis lived in harmony. "For many generations," wrote Plato, "their hearts were true and in all ways noble, and they showed gentleness joined with wisdom."

A Dreadful Day of Reckoning

At the height of Atlantis's glory, 9,200 years before Plato's birth, the imperial island could claim dominion over most of the Mediterranean. "Then above all," declared Plato, "they appeared to be superlatively fair and blessed." Yet, he continued, the Atlanteans were "filled with lawless ambition and power."

Limitless luxury had taken its toll. No longer did the Atlanteans value goodness above material wealth. "The portion of divinity within them was now becoming faint and weak through being ofttimes blended with a large measure of mortality," Plato said. The Atlanteans, "unable to bear the burden of their possessions," had lost their virtue. And now they were massing armies to conquer Athens and parts east.

But Zeus, leader of the gods, delivered a blow of his own — a punishment that was unimaginably total. "There occurred portentous earthquakes and floods," Plato wrote, "and one grievous day and night befell them, when . . . the island of Atlantis . . . was swallowed up by the sea and vanished." Plato doubted that any sign of the lost land would ever be found. "The ocean at that spot," he wrote, "has now become impassable and unsearchable."

CHAPTER 1

Atlantis: The Eternal Quest

n April 12, 1939, a sixty-two-year-old man sank into a trancelike state and spoke of the last days of a long-lost world. If his thoughts were disjointed, his meaning was as clear as it was startling. "In Atlantis," he said, "when there was the breaking up of the land, came to what was called the Mayan land or what is now Yucatan—entity was the first to cross the water in the plane or air machine of that period."

The speaker was Edgar Cayce, known as the sleeping prophet because he invariably experienced his visions in a seeming stupor. For two decades, this enigmatic, unlettered American seer would astound listeners with confidently detailed pronouncements about the fabled island continent of Atlantis. Hailed as a greatly gifted clairvoyant and healer, Cayce told of an ancient place that, before it was swallowed by the ocean, had produced technological marvels not to be seen again until the twentieth century. He spoke of living men and women who, in earlier incarnations, had been citizens of this vanished continental nation. He recounted how survivors of the final cataclysm had fanned out by various means—some on board Atlantean aircraft—to bear remnants of their knowledge and achievements to nearly all the corners of the globe.

To be sure, Cayce painted an incredible picture. As one of his sons would later say of the Atlantis tales: "They are the most fantastic, the most bizarre, the most impossible information in the Edgar Cayce files." Another son, namesake Edgar Evans Cayce, put it a different—and more hopeful—way. "Unless proof of the existence of Atlantis is one day discovered," he conceded, "Edgar Cayce is in a very unenviable position. On the other hand, if he proves accurate on this score he may become as famous an archeologist or historian as he was a medical clairvoyant."

However improbable they may appear, Cayce's chronicles of Atlantis cannot fail to fascinate. For the lost continent remains tightly woven into the fabric of the human heritage, a land that has tantalized philosophers and poets, historians and schemers, scientists and explorers for more than two millennia, ever since the Greek philosopher Plato described it in his writings 355 years before the birth of Christ. The story of Atlantis has spoken to generation after generation about the power and wisdom of the ancients. It is a recollection of

Eden, of a paradise resting now in the dragon-green depths of the sea. Human ambitions may vault beyond the earth to the moon and planets and even to the most distant stars, but memories of that wondrous continent still persist—and not alone in the strange revelations of Edgar Cayce.

The world is filled with mysterious sites, regions, and structures that excite the imagination and lead to speculation about their origins and purposes. Some, such as Atlantis and the secret innards of the earth, are unseen, perhaps existing only in the minds of believers; others are highly visible but inscrutable nonetheless. There is the Great Pyramid of Cheops at Giza—a monument to an Egyptian god-king, certainly, but perhaps far more than that. There are the awesome columns and archways of Britain's Stonehenge, built by unknown hands as a device for tracking the cycle of the sun but possibly invested with other meanings too. On the coastal desert of Peru, lengthy lines and vast figures of animals and humanlike creatures have been etched into the arid ground—drawings that can best be seen in their entirety from high above. What do they signify? How, for that matter, did their makers even perceive them whole?

Such markings, monuments, and locales often have been explained in ways that range from the wholly imaginative to the mundane, from the poetic to the scientific. They continue to be grist for the doubter and the true believer, the charlatan and the honestly curious. And of all the mystic places, the most enigmatic—and the source of many of the rest, in the view of some people—is the lost island continent of Atlantis. The subject of more than 2,000 books and countless articles and poems, Atlantis

has been traced to a long list of sites and regions in the world, among them most of the oceans and continents, to mountain ranges such as the Atlas Mountains of North Africa, to deserts such as the Sahara, to islands such as Malta in the Mediterranean and Bimini in the Caribbean, to cities such as Carthage on the Gulf of Tunis and Cádiz in southwest Spain. The supposed civilization of Atlantis, long vanished from the earth, has been hailed for spawning a number of other known civilizations, including those of Hellenic Greece, the Mayas and Incas of the New World, and even ancient Egypt. It has also been linked to the high cultures of two other allegedly lost continents, Mu and Lemuria.

The first known account of Atlantis was supplied by the great Greek thinker Plato, who lived from about 428 to 348 B.C. A student of the philosopher Socrates, Plato formed his own school of philosophy in the groves of Academe in Athens. He wrote out his philosophy in the form of dialogues—playlets that featured his former teacher Socrates as the main character. Such is the case in *The Republic,* the dialogue in which Socrates and his interlocutors work out their ideal philosophy of government, a benign despotism of philosopher-kings.

Apparently, Plato tried but failed to persuade the ruler of Syracuse—in what is now Sicily—to adopt his political philosophy. Then, late in life, he composed two more dialogues that picked up where *The Republic* had left off. It is in these, *Timaeus* and *Critias,* written around 355 B.C. when Plato was in his seventies, that the earliest surviving description of the lost continent appears.

Plato's Timaeus, one of the original characters in *The Republic,* was an astronomer; most of the dialogue named for him deals

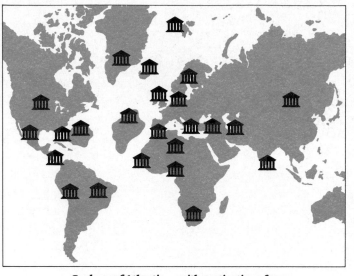

Seekers of Atlantis — with motivations from scientific curiosity to nationalism — have claimed evidence of the island in numerous places, as shown on this map.

with what was then known about the natural world and its origins. The dialogue is written as if it had occurred the day after the conversation that makes up *The Republic;* before Timaeus speaks about the natural sciences, another remarkable discussant, Critias the historian, says that he knows of a place where the philosophy of governance had been just as proposed in *The Republic.* The story of that privileged locale, Critias explains, had been passed down to him from relatives by word of mouth and a few scribbled notes by the Greek statesman Solon, who had heard it a century and a half earlier from Egyptian priests.

According to the Egyptians, the place that matched the ideals of *The Republic* was none other than Athens. But it had been an Athens of a much earlier time—some 9,000 years before, in fact. There, Athena, the goddess of wisdom, had established a city that would produce "men of the greatest wisdom" and, as it turned out, courage. For beyond the Pillars of Hercules (the Strait of Gibraltar), there was a threatening island larger than northern Africa and Asia Minor combined— that is, a continent equal in size to most of the known world in Plato's day. On the island continent, "a great and marvelous power" had arisen. This was Atlantis, and its kings had extended their influence well into the Mediterranean as far as central Italy and Egypt. The Atlanteans, in fact, were "arrogantly" seeking control of all the world. Then the Athenian warriors defeated the armies of Atlantis in a great battle, and the city's leaders liberated all those east of the Pillars of Hercules. But on the heels of this glorious victory came violent earthquakes and floods that destroyed the early Athenians and sank the entire continent of Atlantis under the sea, all in a devastating period of a day and a night.

Such catastrophes, the Egyptian priest had informed Solon, were certainly common enough in the world. But the Greeks had lost the early records of their history. Egypt, thanks to the valve action of its regularly flooding Nile River, was

protected from such disasters; thus, it still retained knowledge of ancient cataclysms. With that brief mention of an early war, Atlantis became a tantalizing part of the historical record. But it remained for Critias, in the dialogue named for him, to describe Atlantis in detail. Indeed, the very quantity and quality of information in *Critias* has given Plato's account of Atlantis much of its enduring plausibility. Critias's report is filled with architectural, engineering, and ceremonial detail that would hardly have been needed if all Plato had in mind was to create a parable or legend to help him make a philosophical point. Moreover, Plato laced the dialogue of *Critias* with uncharacteristic references to the tale as "the realm of fact" and "genuine history." And Solon, who supposedly brought the story back to Greece, was a real person who had actually visited Egypt as a statesman. All in all, Plato took great pains to make his record of Atlantis seem credible to the readers of his time, and that tone of certainty has remained a challenge for more than 2,000 years.

Today, of course, few people believe in Poseidon, the Greek sea-god, or in any of the rest of the Hellenic pantheon. But when Critias resumed his account of Atlantis, he quite naturally spoke in terms of divine origins. In the earliest times, he explained, when the gods were dividing the earth among themselves, Poseidon chose the fair and bounteous continent and subsidiary islands that would come to be known as Atlantis. There, with a woman named Cleito, he sired five sets of twin sons; the firstborn child was Atlas, for whom the continent and the surrounding ocean were named.

Poseidon divided Atlantis into ten parts, granting Atlas the biggest and best portion and making him sovereign over his brothers, who were made rulers over the remaining provinces. Atlantis was a land of bountiful plains, extensive stands of timber, and a rich flora and fauna, including great herds of elephants. The ground was seamed with the ore of gold, silver, and other metals, including a mysterious one called orichal-

The inner city of Atlantis, as described by Plato and depicted in this schematic view, was ringed: It spread out from a hill across three belts of water and two of land. Spanning the canals was an avenue leading from the outer city.

From Myth to Reality

Like the story of Atlantis, the tale of high-walled Troy and its destruction was long held to be a myth. The epic poems describing the city, Homer's *Iliad* and *Odyssey,* are ancient; the great Greek poet created them before 700 B.C. Although classical Greeks read Homer as history, later scholars consigned him to the ranks of literature, conceived in an age of fantasy.

It took Heinrich Schliemann, a nineteenth-century millionaire, amateur archeologist, and dreamer, to prove the scholars wrong. Stubborn and romantic, the German-born businessman *(right)* became convinced that Homer had told the truth about Troy. In the late 1860s, Schliemann decided that the Turkish town of Hissarlik, known for its fortresslike earth mounds, best matched the scene of the *Iliad.* In 1871, he began to dig.

Soon he found that a city did indeed lie beneath Hissarlik's earthworks. In fact, several stages of an ancient city were buried there, one atop the other. And one of the layers, scorched by fire, looked very much like Homer's Troy.

The excavation reached its climax on a morning in the summer of 1873.

That day, Schliemann prized golden necklaces, earrings, dishes, and more out of the hard-packed earth. He would later place the most spectacular piece, a gold diadem, on the brow of his Greek wife, Sophia *(above, far right),* dubbing her "my Helena."

Schliemann's discovery made him famous. Subsequent archeologists have confirmed that the city he unearthed is very probably Troy, albeit a Troy that underwent drastic change through the centuries. And the German businessman's conversion of a myth into reality continues to give hope to the idealists who search for signs of that other place of Greek legend, Atlantis.

Greek soldiers haul their treacherous gift, a wooden horse filled with warriors, to the gates of Troy (left) in this eighteenth-century painting by G. D. Tiepolo.

cum—a copper that Plato wrote "sparkled like fire." At the southern end of the continent, the kings built a city of a magnificence to match the great power that so rich a land soon achieved. This city, also called Atlantis, consisted of concentric rings of land and waterways.

In the center, on a high hill where Poseidon and Cleito had conceived Atlas and his twin brother, the Atlanteans raised a great temple to Poseidon, with a statue of the god riding a golden chariot through the sea in the company of dolphins. In the city, there were springs, both hot and cold, some for the use of the kings, others for the citizens, still others for the beasts of burden. The outer rings held a racecourse and houses for the citizens. The inner harbors were filled with the vessels of war.

For generations, the ten kings ruled their respective domains, abiding always by the firm laws set down long before by Poseidon. At alternate intervals of five and six years, the monarchs would meet together and perform a long and complex ceremony in which a wild bull, captured with a noose, was sacrificed and its blood allowed to course down over sacred bronze columns in the temple. Afterward, the kings donned sacred dark robes and discussed among themselves any transgressions between kingdoms that might have occurred in the interval since the last assembly. They inscribed the results of these deliberations on tablets of gold.

It was not long before Atlantis—gifted with wealth, strength, and internal harmony—began to extend its power outward. But at the same time, the divine and virtuous character of its populace had begun to weaken with the passage of years. "Human nature," Critias reported, "got the upper hand." The Atlanteans began to exhibit less seemly qualities: Uncurbed ambition, greed and ugliness grew among the citizens and their rulers as well. Perceiving that an "honorable race was in a woeful plight," Critias said, Zeus summoned the gods to determine what punishment to inflict on Atlantis. "And when he had called them together he spoke as follows:"

And this is where Critias breaks off. For unknown reasons, Plato ended his chronicle of Atlantis before he had given the details—only touched upon in the earlier dialogue of Timaeus—of the war with the Athenians and the terrible earthquake and floods that sank the once-blessed continent into the depths of the sea.

Despite Plato's best efforts to make Atlantis seem real, his descriptive account was soon the subject of controversy. Even his student Aristotle claimed that Plato had fabricated the Atlantis story and contrived the continent's catastrophic demise as a literary convenience. For many centuries thereafter, scholarship in the Western world was based on the reading of texts by the greats of earlier times, and philosophers generally aligned themselves in schools of thought that were either Aristotelian or Platonic. The Platonists claimed that Plato's account of Atlantis was straight history, while Aristotelians took the opposite point of view and maintained that the lost continent was pure myth.

Even so, it was easy enough to believe that a mysterious land might once have existed in the fastness of the Atlantic. The seas beyond the Strait of Gibraltar remained largely unexplored and, in the minds and maps of men, were perilously laced with reefs and shallows, not to mention strange and dangerous creatures. There were plenty of corroborative stories about other Atlantic landforms—Ogygia in the epics of the Greek poet Homer, for instance—that lent credence to the Platonic account of the lost continent. And here and there in old texts was circumstantial evidence for those predisposed to believe it. For example, in an offhand comment about the geographical distribution of seals, a second-century Roman naturalist named Claudius Aelianus had written that the royalty of Macedonia, like the king of Atlantis, had worn headbands adorned with the image of a ram seal. Presumably, the real-life Macedonians had adopted this emblem in emulation of equally substantial Atlanteans.

During the period known as the Dark Ages, however, European scholars turned their attention almost exclusively from worldly matters to theology and the business of the Church. Atlantis was, for many centuries, a matter of relatively small concern. But with the coming of the Renaissance, many thinkers returned hungrily to the classic texts of Greece and Rome, and there, once again, they found Atlantis. Meanwhile,

seafarers probed the great ocean to the west. Sometimes their journeys spawned legends: For example, in the thirteenth century, the Irish monk Saint Brendan sailed west in search of paradise, purportedly encountered sea monsters and demonic beings, and discovered the Isles of the Blest—which took their various places on generations of maps. By the time Columbus set sail, map makers had endowed the Atlantic Ocean with numerous other islands both real and imagined—among them Avalon, the fabled land where King Arthur was said to have gone after receiving mortal wounds at the battle of Camlan. Close by were the Azores and the Canaries, lying only a few hundred miles off the coast of North Africa; some scholars believe that these islands may be the mountainous remnants of a sunken land.

When the New World burst upon the European consciousness, the Americas quickly became prime candidates for the location of Atlantis. A Spaniard, Francesca Lopez de Gomara, first made the suggestion in 1553, and Sir Francis Bacon adopted it when he wrote *The New Atlantis,* a utopian novel. But the origins of Atlantis were also sought elsewhere—often with the spirit of chauvinism inherent in the rise of European nationalism. In 1675, Olof Rudbeck, a Swedish scholar, used Homeric sailing directions to Ogygia and located Atlantis in Sweden. The English poet William Blake believed that the Atlantean King Albion led the last of his subjects to Britain, where they became Druids. Ancient Egyptians, Goths, and Scyths were all seen to be escapees from doomed Atlantis, and the discovery of blue eyes and blondness among some of Africa's Berbers soon led some people to place Atlantis in the Atlas Mountains of modern Morocco and Tunisia. The paradisiacal continent was also identified as part of an ancient series of land bridges that stretched across the Atlantic and even out into the Pacific as far as New Zealand.

As time passed and geographical knowledge grew, such notions began to look increasingly farfetched. Even students of Plato had their doubts about the whole thing: In 1841, the French scholar T. Henri Martin wrote a commentary on *Timaeus* and called Atlantis pure fiction. The geography of Europe, Asia, and Africa, he pointed out, showed none of the profound effects that would have followed the cataclysmic disappearance of an Atlantis-size landmass; neither were there any shallows where the continent was supposed to have been. Martin concluded that the search for Atlantis was a futile cause; the vanished continent, he said, was truly a utopia—which means, literally, no place.

With Martin's authoritative broadside, Atlantis might well have been banished roundly to the realm of myth, never again to be put forward as a real place. But within a few decades, the lost continent found a new and eloquent champion—and a highly unlikely one at that.

Ignatius Loyola Donnelly was a man of many dreams and ambitions. Born in Philadelphia in 1831, he was the son of an impoverished Irish immigrant who had abandoned his academic studies for the Roman Catholic priesthood, become a shopkeeper, and then gone on to study medicine. Donnelly's mother worked as a pawnbroker to help put her husband through medical school.

Unfortunately for the growing Donnelly family, the freshly minted physician contracted typhus from a patient and died just two years after starting his medical practice. Donnelly's strong-willed mother, six months pregnant at the time, never remarried but devoted herself to raising her children. She was a strict disciplinarian who encouraged her offspring to excel; her daughters would later joke that their mother had shattered many a pair of eyeglasses with her piercing looks.

Following his graduation from the prestigious and demanding Central High School—where he lived up to his mother's expectations by reading widely and developing a striking talent for writing poetry and prose—the short, red-haired Ignatius Donnelly hired on as a clerk for an up-and-coming Philadelphia lawyer. After three years, qualified to be a lawyer himself, Donnelly set up his own practice. Drawn into Democratic politics, he soon made his mark as an orator and drew praise from the powerful Senator John C. Breckinridge.

Despite his budding career as a Philadelphia politician, Donnelly continued to nurse a long-standing dream of opportunity in the West. In 1856, after checking out the prospects in several western states and territories, he left the city of his birth and moved with his new wife to Minnesota. There he took up with a fellow Philadelphian named John Nininger in promoting a prospective metropolis that was grandly dubbed Nininger City. He also dabbled in local Republican politics.

His Nininger City scheme was ultimately a failure, but Donnelly's political career blossomed. A spellbinding speaker, he stumped the state in 1859 and was elected lieutenant governor. Three years later, he won a seat in the United States Congress. After a second term, he ran afoul of post-Civil War political turmoil and lost his bid for reelection. For the next decade and more, Donnelly remained active in Minnesota politics; in 1878, he made another bid for Congress — this time as a Democrat. Defeated in a hard-fought campaign, he contested the outcome and spent most of the following two years gathering evidence and presenting his case in Washington. But as 1880 drew to a close, he realized that he was fighting a losing battle. On November 3, his forty-ninth birthday, Donnelly complained in his diary: "All my hopes are gone, and the future settles down upon me dark and gloomy indeed." In fact, his future was about to take a new and different turn.

Donnelly had been a voracious reader ever since his days at Central High School. His diverse interests ranged from archeology and geology to linguistics and history. During his off-hours as a congressman in Washington, he had often strolled to the Library of Congress to study the latest books and journals in these fields. Then, sometime in the 1870s—possibly after reading Jules Verne's wildly popular novel, *Twenty Thousand Leagues under the Sea,* in which submarine explorers come upon the remains of drowned Atlantis—Donnelly developed an abiding fascination for the lost continent. With that, his previously random studies took on a distinct focus; in nearly everything he read, he seemed to find echoes of a long-vanished civilization.

Now, back home in Minnesota, his political ambitions in tatters, Donnelly turned for solace to his dreams of Atlantis. By mid-January of 1881, he could note more cheerfully in his diary that he was beavering away on a book of his own, a book

This invitation to an 1883 Mardi Gras ball, featuring Atlanteans amid a pantheon of gods, is an example of the craze touched off by Donnelly's theories about Atlantis.

that he called simply *Atlantis*. When he was not at work in the comfortable, book-filled study of his Nininger City house, Donnelly could often be found at D. D. Merrill's well-stocked bookstore in nearby St. Paul. There he picked up the latest scientific journals and bought volume after volume on history, geography, mythology, and world literature. Reading and writing at a furious pace, laboring long into the night by the glow of kerosene lamps, Donnelly became more convinced than ever that Plato's Atlantis had existed—and just where Plato had said it was. He further concluded that Atlanteans were the first men to achieve civilization and that the deities of various ancient mythologies were in fact the actual royalty of Atlantis. As Donnelly saw it, refugees from Atlantis had fanned out around the world and created many civilizations—in Egypt (the world of the pharaohs was a virtual dead ringer for Atlantean civilization, according to Donnelly), in India, in Central America, and elsewhere. Indeed, Donnelly attributed a great deal more to Atlantis than had Plato or any other commentator.

In poring over scientific literature, Donnelly found no shortage of authorities whose writings seemed to bolster his own notions. Scientists of the day knew, for example, of what would later be called the Mid-Atlantic Ridge, a volcano-dotted fracture stretching north and south through the Atlantic seabottom. Sir Charles Lyell, the leading geologist of the nineteenth century, had observed in his landmark *Principles of Geology* that a group of islands arising at some future time along that line would acquire inestimable commercial and political influence. Upon reading that, Donnelly required no great leap of the imagination to envision such influential islands de-

scending as well as arising along the same fracture.

Donnelly also found corroboration for his developing Atlantis theories in the world of botany. The German botanist Otto Kuntze, for example, had written that the principal domesticated tropical plants of Asia and the Americas were of the same species. Kuntze cited especially the banana, which required an extended period of intelligent and determined cultivation to achieve its seedless domestic form. For Donnelly, the message was clear: The banana had first been cultivated in Atlantis, then transplanted to its modern habitats. He saw a like explanation for the similarities that paleontologists were finding between the prehistoric animal life of Europe and America.

More important for his thesis, Donnelly discerned far too many similarities between widely separated cultures to be explainable as mere coincidence. As his research led him to deluge legends from Asian civilizations, American Indian cultures, and the ancient civilizations of the Middle East, Donnelly totally rejected the possibility that such kindred stories could have arisen by chance. The only possible explanation for so universal a concept, he concluded, had to be a single source—the lost continent of Atlantis—from which the tale of deluge had spread, changing slightly but not importantly through centuries of oral transmission.

This sort of pattern loomed wherever Donnelly looked. A favored symbol of the Bronze Age, he found, was the spiral. And spiral images cropped up at old sites in Scotland, in Switzerland, and in the rock-face carvings of the Zuni Indians in New Mexico. On a far larger scale, Donnelly contemplated the similarities between the pyramids of Egypt and those in Teotihuacán in Mexico; even the mysterious mounds scattered throughout the Mississippi Valley were pyramidal. In ancient Nineveh, each of the heavenly bodies was represented by a color—the moon by silver, for example; Donnelly ferreted out a custom in England, still observed during his time, of greeting the new moon by "turning one's silver." And when he made an examination of illustrations of Mycenean arches, he noted that they looked for all the world like those in the Central American site of Palenque.

Even in linguistics, the murkiest area of all, Donnelly perceived analogues that suggested a common origin of the world's languages. And he piled up example after example: The Chinese word for "brick" was *ku*; the Chaldean word for "brick" was *ke*. For "cloth," both used the word *sik*. Finding evidence that variants of a single mother tongue ran from Iceland to Ceylon, he went on to write that a wider generalization was reasonable: "There is abundant proof—proof with which pages might be filled—that there was a still older mother-tongue . . . the language of Noah, the language of Atlantis, the language of the great 'aggressive empire' of Plato."

Writing at a feverish pace, Donnelly completed his book in mid-March of 1881. He titled the finished product *Atlantis: The Antedeluvian World.* Soon afterward, armed with letters of introduction from his St. Paul bookseller, he traveled to New York to make the rounds of the major publishers. His number one choice was Harper and Brothers, and he was overjoyed when editors at that distinguished firm agreed at first reading to publish the book and, more important, to promote it.

Donnelly's *Atlantis* went on sale in early 1882. Not even the enthusiastic author was fully prepared for the acclaim it elicited. Early reviews called it "plausible, perspicuous, buttressed by many curious and recondite facts" and suggested that it was one of the notable books of the century. William Gladstone, Great Britain's prime minister at the time, read the book and wrote Donnelly a glowing letter. Wearing ripped pants and a nearly buttonless coat, Donnelly sat in Nininger City reading Gladstone's letter and wrote in his diary: "I looked down at myself, and could not but smile at the appearance of the man who, in this little, snow-bound hamlet, was corresponding with the man whose word was fate anywhere in the British Empire."

Donnelly's vision of the lost continent found an immense audience. New Orleans would devote its Mardi Gras celebration the next year to the theme of Atlantis, and so great was the book's reception in America and abroad that its author was elected to membership in the American Association for the Advancement of Science. *Atlantis* was soon available in translation throughout Europe, and many people on both sides of the Atlantic were thoroughly convinced by Donnelly's marshaling of evidence from science, literature, religion, folklore, and mythology.

But his account was, in a sense, a legal brief, with all the virtues and vices of lawyerly pleading. Caught up with his argument, Donnelly seized upon any scrap of evidence, however circumstantial, that would bolster his case. He did not always seek confirmation of the curious facts he unearthed, and he ignored contradictory information. In addition, he garbled such things as Bronze Age chronology to suit his purpose. As a result, scientists, accustomed to more rigorous research and presentation, were not especially taken with his conclusions. Charles Darwin, father of the theory of biological evolution—whose work was cited by Donnelly—read *Atlantis* in what he reported to be a "very skeptical spirit."

Indeed, Donnelly himself knew that his argument was incomplete. What he needed to clinch the case for Atlantis was tangible evidence. As Donnelly said at the end of his book: "A single engraved tablet dredged up from Plato's island would be worth more to science, would more strike the imagination of mankind, than all the gold of Peru, all the monuments of Egypt, and all the terra-cotta fragments gathered from the great libraries of Chaldea."

Whatever the scholarly shortcomings of Donnelly's carefully crafted *Atlantis,* it sold hugely for years. By 1890, the United States market had gobbled up twenty-three editions, and twenty-six had appeared in England. A major reason for such widespread interest in an ancient, lost civilization was that

Searching for City X

Of the many explorers who have sought traces of Atlantis, none was more intrepid than Colonel Percy Harrison Fawcett. A self-proclaimed lone wolf, the determined British army surveyor spent the early years of this century mapping the jungles of Ceylon and South America. In 1908, he led a team *(above, with Fawcett seated front and center)* that surveyed the border between Brazil and Bolivia. By 1925, retired from the army, he was ready for an ambitious expedition of his own: the search for a legendary ruined city in the jungles of Brazil.

Fawcett's interest in lost civilizations was spurred by a black stone idol, carved with mysterious characters, that adventure writer Sir H. Rider Haggard had given him. Haggard said the ten-inch statue had been found in Brazil. Fawcett consulted with a psychic reader to discover the idol's source and was told that it came from "a large irregularly shaped continent stretching from the north coast of Africa across to South America." The explorer was

persuaded that his enigmatic artifact had traveled from that continent — clearly Atlantis — to an Atlantean colony deep within Brazil.

Fawcett was encouraged in this belief when he acquired an old map showing a nameless city in the little-known Mato Grosso area of southwest Brazil. Accompanied only by his son Jack and his son's friend Raleigh Rimell, the adventurer set forth into the jungle in search of the place he called City

X. Then, after writing to his wife about rumors of an ancient metropolis on a lake, Fawcett and his two young companions disappeared. Their remains were never found.

Yet as legend at least, Percy Fawcett lived on. For decades afterward, South American travelers related tales of gaunt old men, seen along jungle pathways, who called themselves Fawcett. Some said they had met blue-eyed, part-Indian children fathered by the adventurers. Others reported that Fawcett had found the idyllic City X and refused to leave.

But the most remarkable account of the explorer to reach the outside world involved the Irish medium and psychic Geraldine Cummins *(inset)*, who claimed in 1936 that she was receiving mental messages from Fawcett. Cummins said the Englishman had found relics of Atlantis in the jungle but was now ill and semiconscious. After four such messages, "Fawcett" fell silent until 1948. In that year, he reported his own death.

a great wave of spiritualism was under way in both Europe and America. Mediums regularly conducted well-attended séances at which they appeared to summon the spirits of the dead and perform a variety of other supernatural acts. It was easy enough to believe that there were unseen powers at work in the world, that events were frequently the results of causes science could not plumb. The occult was very much a part of nineteenth-century culture. Taking comfort, perhaps, from the scholarly trappings of Donnelly's book, occultists churned out a profusion of elaborations on the Atlantis theme.

Indeed, there had already been a fair amount of such speculation when Donnelly sat down in his library in Nininger City to write *Atlantis.* And some of it had involved lost continents undreamed of by Plato. In 1864, for example, a French scholar and cleric named Charles-Etienne Brasseur de Bourbourg was studying at a library in Madrid when he came across a treatise that contained a key to the complex alphabet used by the vanished Mayan civilization of Central America. Thus armed, Brasseur set out to translate one of the few Mayan manuscripts that had survived destruction by sixteenth-century Spanish conquistadors.

As Brasseur pored over the elaborately embellished Mayan text, painstakingly deciphering its intricate symbols, he discovered the story of an ancient land that had sunk into the ocean after a catastrophic volcanic eruption. Finding a pair of mysterious figures that evidently corresponded to the letters *M* and *U* in the modern alphabet, Brasseur determined that the continent had been named Mu.

Other scholars were skeptical; their attempts with the key produced nonsense translations. But French archeologist Augustus le Plongeon, who had been the first to excavate Mayan ruins, used the alphabet key and other symbols from Mayan walls to come up with an elaborate account of

Brasseur's continent. According to le Plongeon's chronicle, a rivalry between two brothers for the hand of Mu's queen—named Moo—led to the death of one brother and a takeover of the country by the other. Just as the continent began to sink following these dramatic events, Queen Moo fled to Egypt. There, as the goddess Isis, she built the Sphinx and founded Egyptian civilization. Other survivors of the catastrophe on Mu escaped to Yucatan, where they wrote down their history and erected great temples.

Mu, which Brasseur and le Plongeon located in the Gulf of Mexico and western Caribbean, bore a striking resemblance to Atlantis. Like Plato's lost continent, Mu comprised ten separate kingdoms. And it had perished, according to the Mayan records, some 8,000 years earlier, at about the same time that, according to Plato, Atlantis was destroyed.

Reports of yet another erstwhile landmass had been inspired by Charles Darwin's theory of evolution, which sought to explain, among other things, why species of plants and animals are located where they are. Noting that lemurs—small, evolutionary predecessors of the monkey—were abundant on the island of Madagascar, off the east coast of southern Africa, and also in small numbers in India and southern Africa itself, scientists suggested that there had once been a continent-size land bridge joining these areas. An English zoologist, Philip Sclater, called this lost land Lemuria. That notion was supported by many prominent scientists of the time, among them Alfred Russel Wallace—who had developed on his own a theory of evolution similar to Darwin's. A German naturalist, Ernst Heinrich Haeckel, went even further, maintaining that the

Wearing full Masonic regalia, French archeologist Augustus le Plongeon strikes a somber pose. His excavations of Mayan ruins in the 1880s convinced him that refugees from Mu, a lost continent resembling Atlantis, had founded the Mayan civilization.

A Vision of Eden

In 1926, an elderly Anglo-American caused a sensation with the publication of his first book, *The Lost Continent of Mu.* In this remarkable treatise, Colonel James Churchward claimed to have found irrefutable evidence linking the biblical Garden of Eden to the legendary sunken Pacific continent of Mu.

Churchward wrote that an old Asian priest had taught him to translate the primordial Muvian language, inscribed on certain tablets in India and Mexico. These tablets confirmed that Mu had been the fountainhead of civilization, predating even Atlantis. Several races of early humans had sprung up there, sharing the country with fauna ranging from brilliant butterflies to mastodons — as shown in Churchward's own illustration *(right)*.

Unfortunately, Churchward reported, this idyllic land rested on a foundation of gas-filled caves. The gas exploded in a great cataclysm 12,000 years ago, and Mu sank beneath the waves. The lucky survivors who escaped to Muvian colonies around the world later inscribed the tablets that Churchward claimed to have deciphered.

No such accounts have ever been found by others, nor have geologists discovered any trace of a sunken Pacific continent. But this has not deterred Churchward's readers: His first and subsequent books on Mu remained in print well into the 1960s.

sunken Lemuria was the evolutionary cradle not only of lemurs but of humankind. This would explain, he said, what was then known about the early geographical distribution of Homo sapiens and would also account for the lack of fossil remains of the evolutionary steps between apes and humans.

Although first proposed as a result of scholarly and scientific speculation, the new continents of Mu and Lemuria quickly caught the fancy of occultists, who proceeded to make far more extravagant claims for the allegedly lost continents. In the 1870s, for example, a British-American researcher named James Churchward began what would become a lifelong investigation of Mu, which he maintained was located in the mid-Pacific. Churchward, citing a chronicle purportedly taken from secret tablets discovered in India, said Mu had been the site of the Garden of Eden and had a population of 64 million people at the time of its destruction about 12,000 years ago *(page 27)*. But Lemuria attracted the most attention, thanks to the prodigious writings of an irrepressible and flamboyant woman who was born in Russia in 1831—coincidentally enough, in the same year as Ignatius Donnelly.

Helena Petrovna Hahn was a beautiful child with dark hair and exceptionally bright blue eyes. Early in life, she showed a marked interest in fantasy and make-believe. Among other things, she assured playmates that she was accompanied on her wanderings through the labyrinthine cellars of her family home by invisible companions that she called her "hunchbacks." She frequently walked and talked in her sleep, and she was such a skillful storyteller that she was said to cause hallucinations in other children who listened as she spun her vivid tales. She was also headstrong: Just weeks before her seventeenth birthday, she married one Nikifor Blavatsky, a government official who was around three times her age. It was a short-lived union. Helena left Blavatsky within months and subsequently married again. But she would style herself forever after as Madame Blavatsky.

Still in her teens, she embarked on a series of global travels and adventures that would occupy her for a lifetime.

Later, she would claim that her journeys had included a seven-year stay in Tibet, where she studied the ancient wisdom of the Hindus. Each time she returned to her home in Russia, family members noticed that she was plumper — eventually she reached about 230 pounds — and perhaps more madcap. She had a boisterous sense of humor, great energy, and a talent for profanity. Everywhere she went, people were captivated by her magnetic personality.

In the 1870s, Madame Blavatsky visited the United States at the height of the same spiritualist craze that would make the public so receptive to Ignatius Donnelly's vision of Atlantis. In New York, she teamed up with a psychic investigator named Henry Steel Olcott in order to form an organization called the Theosophical Society, after the Greek words for "god" and "wisdom." A stated purpose of the society, which soon attracted numerous adherents, was to look into ancient mysteries, such as the secrets of the pyramids and the nature of people of the distant past.

As spiritual head of a growing movement, Madame Blavatsky created for the Theosophical Society a major occult work called *The Secret Doctrine,* completed in 1888. In this landmark, two-volume book, Madame Blavatsky reported that revelatory spirits from the Orient had taught her about the lost continents of Atlantis and Lemuria. She and her disciples subsequently elaborated on the Lemurian continent as part of a universal philosophy drawn from a number of Western and Eastern sources.

According to Madame Blavatsky and her followers, the Lemurians were the third of seven "root" races of mankind. Their continent occupied most of the Southern Hemisphere, and they were originally hermaphrodite people who communicated only by psychic powers conferred upon them by a third eye. The fourth race was the Atlanteans, who evolved from the Lemurians as Lemuria sank beneath the sea millions of years ago; they inhabited a spur of Lemuria in the northern Atlantic that itself was to sink later, finally disappearing about 9,000 years ago. Madame Blavatsky believed refugees from that disaster escaped to Central Asia, where they evolved into modern Hindus and Europeans.

Helena Blavatsky's transfixing gaze reveals the charisma that brought her renown. Among her writings, supposedly inspired by psychic messages, are accounts of Lemurians.

Another enthusiastic chronicler of Atlantis and Lemuria was the Austrian mystic and philosopher Rudolf Steiner. Strongly influenced by the works of Madame Blavatsky and her theosophical disciples, Steiner went on to form his own spiritual movement, which he called Anthroposophy, from the Greek words for man and wisdom. Among other things, the Anthroposophical Society founded a number of schools and promoted organic agriculture.

In his voluminous writings and lectures, Steiner had ready rejoinders for those doubters who would question his conclusions about the lost continents. Once, for example, he noted that Atlantean airships would be inoperable in modern times, having been designed to fly in the much denser atmosphere that he said prevailed during the heyday of Atlantis. Anticipating the responses of his critics, he went on to observe: "We need not raise the question now as to whether such a condition of density is compatible with the opinion held by modern science, for science and logical thought can, owing to their inherent attributes, never say the final word as to what is possible, or impossible."

Steiner also maintained that human bodies, along with rocks and mineral deposits, were somehow softer and more pliable thousands of years ago in Lemurian and Atlantean times than they would later become.

The most elaborate descriptions of the lost continents and their inhabitants were created by the theosophist writer W. Scott-Elliott. According to Scott-Elliott's chronicle, published in 1893, the Atlanteans lived in a nearly totalitarian society ruled by an upper class that had harnessed a great number of technological marvels. For example, they flew about their realms in 100-mile-an-hour airships that were powered by a mysterious fuel known as *vril*, essentially a life-force that produced propulsion in somewhat the same way a modern jet engine does.

Such fanciful details about life in Lemuria and Atlantis—and further elaborations of Mu—have been divined by what their discoverers call occult powers, the reading of psychic memories that somehow survive the passage of eons. Conventional scientists may scoff at such claims, but others have concluded that there are unconventional ways of knowing things. For example, some people say that certain quartz crystals, employed as aids to meditation, can enable the user to tune in to a special kind of benevolent wisdom that was, perhaps, the essence of Atlantis. Still others maintain that the mysteries of Atlantis have never been plumbed so thoroughly as they were in the first half of the twentieth century by Edgar Cayce, that gentle, nearly illiterate psychic healer who told of the lost continent while lying in a sleeplike trance.

Born in 1877, the son of a Kentucky farmer, Edgar Cayce had to leave school in the seventh grade to go to work. Later, he hoped to become a preacher but came down with a throat ailment that reduced his voice to the merest whisper. After doctors failed to cure him, he asked a friend to put him in a hypnotic trance; in this state, Cayce spoke out in a loud, firm voice, diagnosing his problem and prescribing the remedy that ultimately worked. Henceforth, there would be two Edgar Cayces, the "sleeping" and the "waking." For years, until his death in 1945, Cayce spent a great deal of his time submerged in deep trances, seeking the causes of people's physical ailments and disabilities, as well as prescribing cures.

In the 1920s, the sleeping Cayce began to stress the existence of reincarnation, the rebirth of departed souls in new bodies. Often, when tracking a patient's previous lives—in what were known as "life readings" as opposed to readings made for healing purposes—Cayce would allude cryptically to a previous life in Atlantis, calling the spirit from that earlier time an "entity." One subject of a life reading was told: "In Atlantean land . . . entity ruled in pomp and power and in understanding of the mysteries of the application of that often termed the nightside of life, or in applying the universal forces as understood in the period."

A relatively simple man, Cayce was deeply religious and was not widely read. He was sometimes astounded to learn what he had said in a trance state, and the waking Cayce worried for a time about his sleeping counterpart's ideas about reincarnation, fearing that they might be unchristian. In fact, the Atlantean references seemed almost incidental. But like all of Cayce's readings after 1932, when an institute was founded to support his work, they were written down. In 650 different readings that Cayce gave for different people over a period of twenty-one years, a vivid picture of the ancient world of Atlantis emerged. And the picture was remarkably consistent in its own terms: The accumulated fragments do not contradict themselves.

Cayce's Atlantis was right where Plato had said it was, in the Atlantic Ocean. "The position . . . the continent of Atlantis occupied," he said in a reading given in 1932, "is between the Gulf of Mexico on the one hand and the Mediterranean upon the other." It was of continental size, and people lived on it for thousands of years, during which it went through three great catastrophic periods of breakup, the last being about 10,000 years ago, when it disappeared.

Before the end, however, the Atlanteans appeared to have developed a highly advanced civilization that was technologically on a par with the industrialized world of the twentieth century. They were evidently an active, questing people who could, among other things, generate electricity and build aircraft. As Cayce intoned during a life reading given on April 19, 1938: "Entity was what would be in the present the electrical engineer—applied those forces or influences for airplanes, ships, and what you would today call radio for constructive or destructive purposes."

Cayce also spoke cryptically of an Atlantean substance called firestone. Used to generate energy, it has been likened by some to the radioactive materials employed in modern times to produce nuclear power. As Cayce explained in a reading given in 1933—more than a decade before the first public demonstration of atomic energy: "The preparation of this stone was solely in the hands of the initiates at the time; and

Edgar Cayce snaps a self-portrait. In his youth,
Cayce was a professional photographer; his later life was devoted to psychic
readings, in which he predicted the rise of Atlantis.

Sir Gerald's Atlantean Opera

Eternally fascinating, the story of the lost continent Atlantis has been told and retold in history books, novels, films — and even in an operetta. Sir Gerald Hargreaves, a British judge and an amateur composer, wrote the musical *Atalanta: A Story of Atlantis* during World War II, when the tale of a country

patch their warrior Achilles (a tenor) to the island to argue their case. The burly soldier, fresh from assaulting the walls of Troy, fails to convince his audience but succeeds in capturing the heart of tomboyish princess Atalanta (a soprano). He whisks

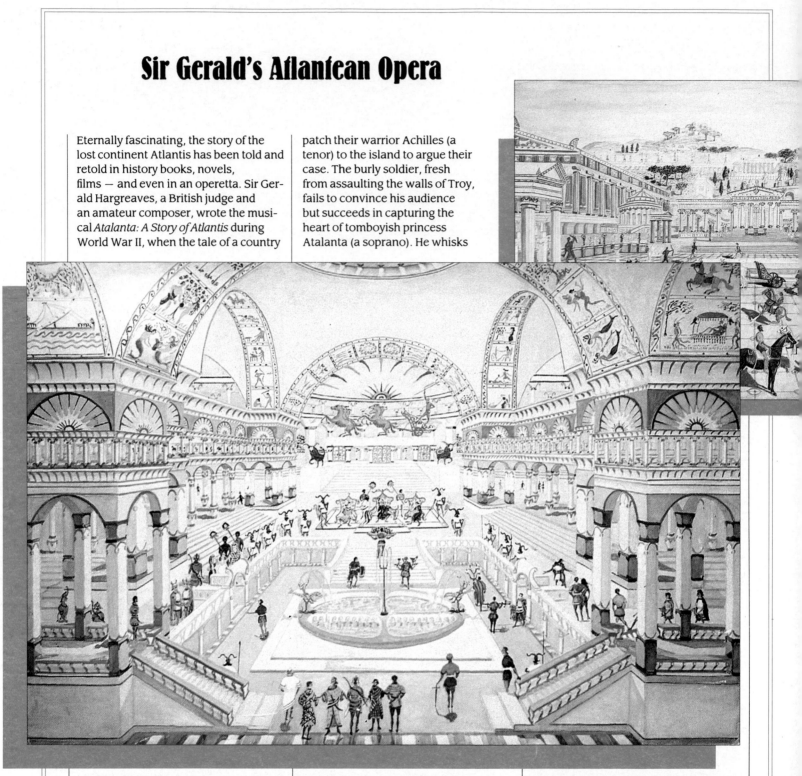

punished for its aggression must have seemed particularly apt.

In a libretto that blends Plato and Homer with Gilbert and Sullivan, Hargreaves shows an Atlantis divided in two factions, one advocating war against Athens, the other pleading for peace. Hearing of this, the Greeks dis-

her away to Greece just as the war-mongers prevail and Atlantis collapses, in four-part harmony, into the sea.

Although Hargreaves's tuneful drama was never produced, the judge made elaborate paintings of several scenes showing his conception of the play. Based on Plato's description of

the island, but liberally embellished, the *Atalanta* stage sets were designed for a monumental production. Those shown here depict the gilded interior of Poseidon's temple *(above)*, a public square in ancient Athens *(above, right)*, and the grandly proportioned rooms at Atlantis's royal palace *(far right)*.

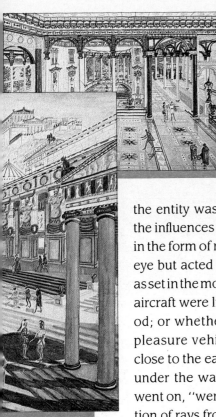

the entity was among those who directed the influences of the radiation which arose, in the form of rays that were invisible to the eye but acted upon the stones themselves as set in the motivating forces—whether the aircraft were lifted by the gases of the period; or whether for guiding the more-of-pleasure vehicles that might pass along close to the earth, or crafts on the water or under the water.'' These vehicles, Cayce went on, ''were impelled by the concentration of rays from the stone which was centered in the middle of the power station.''

According to Edgar Cayce's account, the Atlanteans had originally appeared on earth in spirit form and had only gradually evolved into material beings. This was, it seems, the beginning of the end for Atlantis; the more fleshly its inhabitants became over the generations, the more troubled their civilization. Said the sleeping Cayce in 1937: ''In Atlantean land when there were those disturbing forces—or just previous to the first disturbing forces that brought the first destruction of the continent, through the application of spiritual things for self-indulgence of material peoples.'' A faction called the Sons of Belial finally gained control of Atlantis, mistreating the land's producers and casting them into a kind of slave status. Society—like the land itself—began to fall apart. And Cayce suggested that the cataclysmic end was caused not only by geological upheavals but also by misuse of technology. He said in 1936: ''In Atlantean land just after second breaking up of the land owing to misapplication of divine laws upon those things of nature or of the earth; when there were the eruptions from the second using of those influences that were for man's own development, yet becoming destructive forces to flesh when misapplied.''

In addition to telling of the life and death of Atlantis, Cayce also made a tantalizing prediction. In the late 1960s, he said, the western region of the long-submerged continent would begin to reappear near the Caribbean island of Bimini. And then, in 1968, divers happened to find in the waters just off Bimini what seemed to be a long roadway paved with rectangular blocks of stone. Many believed that the sleeping Cayce's prophecy had come to pass, that this was an actual remnant of the vanished Atlantean civilization. Indeed, radio-carbon dating of the monumental blocks indicated an age of some 12,000 years.

But geologists were quick to point out similar rock formations in Australia and even along the very shore of Bimini itself. Like the 2,000-foot Bimini road, said the scientists, these are not man-made structures; rather, they are the result of the formation of beach rock. In this natural process, the calcium carbonate grains left from the decay of sea creatures wash or blow over sand and become embedded there, forming hard rock. Exposure to the sun and slippage of loose sand from underneath cause the rock to fracture in relatively straight lines along the shore and then at right angles, creating the effect of a road made with craftsmanly precision. As shore-lines change, such formations become submerged and can appear to be ancient thoroughfares.

Undersea roadways are not the only alleged remnants of Atlantis that have been undermined by modern science. Indeed, the continuing precision of twentieth-century geology has been especially unkind to the idea of a long-lost continent resting beneath the sea. The ability to measure the speed of earthquake vibrations as they reverberate around the earth has led geologists to the conclusion that the material that composes the earth's crust under continents is vastly different from that of any ocean basin. And in tracking such vibrations through the ocean floors, geologists have turned up no sign of a large mass of continent-type material.

The theory of continental drift and plate tectonics has also taken its toll on concepts about Atlantis. First proposed in the early years of this century—and scorned for more than a generation—this revolutionary theory has it that all of the world's continents were once joined together in a huge land-mass called Pangaea. Some 200 million years ago they split off and began the slow and continuing movement that has carried them to their present locations. The mechanism that

Dotted with volcanic islets, Thera's harbor shows the outlines of an eruption. Some scientists believe the cataclysm that shattered this Aegean island in 1500 B.C. inspired the tale of Atlantis.

drives the continents—which float on hard crustal plates across the more malleable mantle of the earth—is the constant upsurging of molten material from the earth's interior at such places as the Mid-Atlantic Ridge, where it creates volcanic islands and pushes the plates apart.

The notion of continental drift gained credence among geologists in the late 1960s and is now accepted by virtually all scientists. And while some believers might imagine that the Americas could have been the Atlantean continent of Plato's dialogues because they were once connected to Europe and Africa, this seems highly unlikely. The process of continental drift is almost immeasurably slow, and North America arrived at its approximate current position about 65 million years ago, at a time when dinosaurs still roamed the earth.

For all the naysaying of science, there are those who still hope that the remains of Atlantis have been overlooked by all of the sophisticated surveys of the ocean bottoms. Geological evidence notwithstanding, such optimists cling to their belief that the ancient continent lies somewhere in the murk, its glories obscured in mud. Meanwhile, other scientists have made the strongest case for the material existence of an Atlantis in olden times. They say that Plato may well have had it close to right.

During the rule of the Fourth Dynasty in Egypt, about 2500 B.C., a commercial empire dominated trade throughout the Mediterranean basin. On Crete and on other islands in the nearby Aegean Sea, the people of this empire used their amassed wealth to build huge multistoried temples, to create large cities, to lay out complex waterworks. Their art, on frescoes and pottery, was highly sophisticated—graceful, swirling, bright with gold. But by Plato's time, this civilization had disappeared, leaving behind only fragments of myths, such as the story of the Greek hero Theseus and his adventures with the bull-like Minotaur. Plato had no knowledge of this civilization's accomplishments. Indeed, no one imagined its reality until 1900, when Sir Arthur Evans began excavations at the site of Cnossus on Crete. There he unearthed the stunning remains of what may have been Europe's first civilization. He called it Minoan, after the legendary King Minos.

Then, in 1909, an anonymous letter appeared in the London *Times* suggesting that the Minoan civilization had been the basis of Plato's Atlantis. The writer, who turned out to be K. T. Frost, a professor of classical history at Queen's University in Belfast, later wrote an article elaborating this theme. The point, Frost emphasized, was to look at Minoan Crete from the perspective of the Egyptians of the time—the source of Plato's information. It would have seemed different from anything the Egyptians were familiar with in Africa or the Near East, a great seafaring empire "united by the same sea which divided it from other nations . . . a separate continent with a genius of its own." Further, to the Egyptians, the center of Minoan civilization would appear to be far to the west, even beyond the four pillars that in the Egyptian world view held up the earth. Frost went on to observe that Plato's mention of a great harbor, lavish bathrooms, a stadium, and the sacrifice of the bulls all jibe with actual features of Minoan Crete, as does the capture of the ceremonial bull, which can be seen on pottery from Crete.

But suddenly the power of the Minoans vanished. (Frost

thought this might have been the result of a Greek raid on Crete.) To the Egyptians, perched as they were on the eastern edge of Africa, from which they rarely ventured forth, the disappearance of these exotic merchants at the evident height of their grandeur would have been a great mystery, as if "the whole kingdom had sunk into the sea." It is this picture of a civilization in the West, arisen to glory and abruptly gone, that would have been in the written records of the Egyptian historians. And this is the version that would have reached Plato.

As plausible as this seemed, few people paid Frost's idea much heed. He evidently dropped the subject himself and later died in World War I. But it was not long before Frost's theory received some powerful support.

In 1932, Spyridon Marinatos, a young Greek *ephor,* or keeper of antiquities, stood upon the shore of Crete. As had many archeologists before him, he was puzzling over the sudden and unexplained demise of the Minoan culture. Ancient records said that the great King Minos had used a site called Amnisos on Crete as the harbor town for his capital city of Cnossus. With a total budget of $135, Marinatos had spent the better part of the summer searching around Amnisos, then little more than a sandy strand of shoreline, for signs of a port. As his funds ran out—indeed, on the last day of his seemingly fruitless expedition—Marinatos dug into the sand once more and struck the fragments of a Minoan fresco decorated with lilies. It was more than enough to bring him back to Amnisos to press his search with new vigor. In later digs, Marinatos unearthed an entire harbor town, complete with a royal villa. "But what especially piqued my interest," he wrote later,

"were the curious positions of several huge stone blocks that had been torn from their foundations and strewn toward the sea." During a subsequent effort, he found in the same area a building brimming with pumice in its basement, sure evidence of volcanic eruption.

Seeking the source of that eruption, Marinatos looked northward some seventy miles to Thera and two other Aegean islands that were known to be the remnants of a volcano that had been active around 1500 B.C., just when Minoan civilization blinked out forever. The three islands are all that is left of a large, round island—a caldera, a volcanic maw, that had exploded so violently that the water depth in the crater is more than 1,000 feet.

Wondering if the event could have been violent enough to eliminate—all at once—so great a power as Crete, Marinatos studied records of the volcanic eruption in 1883 of Krakatoa, in the Sunda Strait between Java and Sumatra. This titanic upheaval was heard 2,000 miles away, and it sent walls of water 100 feet high crashing at fifty miles an hour into Java and Sumatra; the rampaging waters charged 1,000 yards inland, sweeping away 300 villages and killing 36,000 people. Marinatos concluded that the eruption of Thera—if it had been as violent as that of Krakatoa—could surely have wiped out the Minoans.

Marinatos reasoned that these kinds of catastrophes, over a long period of prehistory, had given rise to the story of Atlantis that was related by Plato. His colleagues in the scientific community remained skeptical, and further research was cut short by the outbreak of World War II. But once the war ended and the pursuit could resume, a Greek seismologist named A. G. Galanopoulos picked up the

An embossed Minoan cup vividly depicts the struggles of a netted bull. Relics such as this echo Plato's account of Atlantean bull hunts, supporting the theory that Crete, home to the Minoan culture, was Atlantis.

thread that led to Thera. On that crescent-shaped island, Galanopoulos found the ruins of unmistakably Minoan buildings that had been devastated by a volcano. A Hungarian colleague, Peter Hédervári, determined on the basis of collapsed land volume at the sites that the eruption at Thera had in fact been about four times more violent than at Krakatoa. The pumice and ash from such a cataclysm would not only have inundated Crete but would have reached as far as Egypt, about 250 miles distant. It would also have caused torrential rains over a wide area, and locally there would have been so much pumice floating on the sea that the waters would have appeared to be filled with muddy reefs for some time. The tsunami, or tremendous sea wave, resulting from the explosion would have seemed for all the world like a flood when it crashed ashore.

Galanopoulos believed that this catastrophic series of events—which would all have taken place in a matter of days—would surely have been recorded by the Egyptians and associated with the sudden disappearance of the once-ubiquitous Minoans. Hearing the story much later, Solon came up with the description recorded by Plato, who translated the vanished civilization into the lost continent of Atlantis.

Plausible as this reconstruction may have appeared, there remained some difficulties. Plato was specific about when the catastrophe had occurred, placing it 9,000 years before his own time. He was also precise in detailing the size of Atlantis and its features; the capital city was some 300 miles across, far larger than any metropolis of even modern times. Furthermore, Plato had explicitly located Atlantis in the Atlantic Ocean.

Galanopoulos's reconciliation of these disparities was ingenious and simple, the kind of explanation that accords with the scientists' law of Occam's Razor. (Named for the fourteenth-century British philosopher who first proposed it, this law holds that the simplest explanation that fits all the facts is probably the correct one.) Both the Egyptians and the Greeks used ten-based number schemes that were precursors of the modern decimal system. Galanopoulos reasoned that, in translation from Egyptian to Greek, the symbol for every

number greater than 100 mistakenly had the equivalent of one zero added. In that case, all the numbers in Plato's account would fit closely enough. For example, if 9,000 years really means 900 years, then the date of the catastrophe accords almost perfectly with the eruption of Thera in 1500 B.C. Similarly, a city 300 miles across becomes 30 miles across, a reasonable figure. And a series of large and small islands ten times the size of Crete and its neighbors simply would not have fit in the Mediterranean as Plato knew it: In his chronicle of Atlantis, the great philosopher would have had to move the lost continent out of the sea and into the much larger ocean that lay beyond the Pillars of Hercules.

It is not unlikely that numbers could have become so garbled in ancient times. The Egyptian symbols for numbers could easily have been confused by the Greek who carried the Atlantis story from Egypt back to his homeland. And it is not surprising that Plato, entranced by the extraordinary tale of a civilization ending in a blink of time's eye, would set out to use the story in some instructive way.

There are those who are satisfied with this modern, scientific account of that enigmatic civilization and its demise. But others see more in Atlantis than scientists do and maintain that this latest theory is only a rationalization by people with a totally materialist cast of mind. After all, Crete is not, they point out, under water.

They will suggest that perhaps the law of Occam's Razor does not necessarily apply to the complicated affairs of humanity and the human spirit. They will hearken to the words of Edgar Cayce, the sleeping prophet, who spoke of the flight of Atlanteans to Egypt to preserve the archives of their dying land: "These may be found," Cayce said in a past life reading given in 1941, "especially when the house or tomb of records is opened, in a few years from now." Perhaps, they say, there does indeed lie in some Egyptian pyramid an undiscovered sanctum containing papyrus with ancient symbols that point beyond the confines of the Mediterranean, beyond even the confines of what science knows of the human psyche, to the place where a mystic Atlantis still rests in the deep, waiting to give up its age-old secrets.

Realm of Unfathomed Mysteries

Ever since the first seamen set sail thousands of years ago, the vast and capricious oceans have been sources of myth and mystery, places populated with strange creatures and possessed of inexplicable powers. Seafarers everywhere have spun yarns of mermaids — beings that are part fish, part human. The Greeks told of the enchantress Circe, who lured unwary sailors to their doom. Norsemen sang of kraken, 200-foot-long monsters with "sharp scales and flaming eyes" that smashed ships and killed sailors. As late as the eighteenth century, Carolus Linnaeus, the father of modern botany, took kraken seriously. "They say that if they were to lay hold of the largest man of war," he wrote, kraken "would pull it to the bottom" of the sea. Others have thought the sea itself has perilous power. When Christopher Columbus first reached the Sargasso Sea midway across the Atlantic, his superstitious crew feared its thick yellow, brown, and green seaweed would trap them forever.

Far more recent is the fear of the so-called Bermuda Triangle, an amorphous area located somewhere east of Bermuda. One student of the unexplained, Ivan T. Sanderson, postulated that the Bermuda Triangle is one of a dozen areas called vile vortices — another infamous one is the so-called Devil's Sea off the coast of Japan — where little-understood forces are said to cause ships to vanish without a trace. Even airplane pilots flying over these areas have reported malfunctioning gyros, dead radios, visual anomalies, and inexplicable time warps. Some of the mysterious incidents that have occurred at sea are recounted on the following pages.

Riddle of the Mary Celeste

On December 4, 1872, the bark *Dei Gratia* was sailing in the Atlantic east of the Azores when she came upon the brigantine *Mary Celeste*. Both ships had sailed from New York a month before: the *Mary Celeste* with the captain's wife and baby daughter as passengers, the *Dei Gratia* with the captain and his crew of seven aboard.

Clearly there was something badly amiss aboard the *Mary Celeste*. Her sails were tattered and hanging awry. No one stood at the wheel. When crewmen from the *Dei Gratia* went aboard and called out greetings, the only reply was silence. No one could be found.

The lifeboat was gone; apparently it had been launched. The binnacle was knocked out of place and the compass was shattered. The bow of the derelict ship bore six-foot gashes just above the waterline, but otherwise the ship appeared sound and seaworthy.

Below deck was a chilling scene that suggested hurried flight. Toys lay on the captain's bed, as if a child had been interrupted at play. The food supply and cargo were undisturbed. The ship's log remained intact, but its last entry, made nine days earlier, gave no hint of impending trouble.

Why did the captain abandon ship? How did he and his companions vanish without a trace? Could insanity, mutiny, faulty instruments, hijacking, poisoning, tornado, or a disturbance in the sea floor have been involved? The captain of the *Dei Gratia* ordered some of his crewmen to sail the *Mary Celeste* to Gibraltar, where a British Vice Admiralty court of inquiry raised all those questions — and found no answers. More than 100 years later, the *Mary Celeste* is believed by many to have been doomed by the inexplicable evil that lurks in the Bermuda Triangle.

A Royal Encounter with the Flying Dutchman

The predawn sky was clear and the sea calm as the HMS *Inconstant* rounded the coast from Melbourne to Sydney, Australia, on July 11, 1881. Suddenly from the lookout on the forecastle came word of a vessel closing in on the port bow. Officers and crew alike — thirteen in all — crowded the rails to see for themselves.

According to the journals of two royal midshipmen who were aboard, Prince George (later King George V) of England and his brother, Prince Albert Victor, the vessel appeared as "a strange red light as of a phantom ship all aglow." Her "masts, spars and sails stood out in strong relief." But moments later, the apparition vanished and there remained "no vestige nor any sign whatever of any material ship."

The witnesses believed that they had seen the *Flying Dutchman,* the legendary ghost ship that has haunted sailors for centuries. With numerous variations, the legend goes like this: A Dutch captain drove his ship around Cape Horn in a savage gale against the pleas of his terrified crew, who begged him to put into port. The Holy Ghost appeared; the satanic captain fired his pistol and cursed the Lord. For his blasphemy, the captain was condemned to sail the seas for eternity, never to put into port. Sailors say an encounter with the *Flying Dutchman* bodes disaster.

So it was for the HMS *Inconstant.* The royal journals record that later that morning the unlucky lookout fell from the fore-topmast crosstrees and was "smashed to atoms." And upon reaching port, the admiral of the ship was stricken with a fatal illness. It would seem that not even the presence of royalty could stave off the curse of the *Flying Dutchman.*

A Fateful Mission in the Bermuda Triangle

At 2:10 p.m. on December 5, 1945, five Avenger torpedo bombers roared off the runway of the Fort Lauderdale Naval Air Station. Flight instructor Lieutenant Charles G. Taylor was leading thirteen crewmen of Flight 19 on a routine navigational training exercise. But—ominously—the course lay over an area bounded approximately by Bermuda, Florida, and Puerto Rico, in what is now known as the Bermuda Triangle, where so many ships and aircraft have met mysterious fates.

Flight 19 began smoothly enough. But at 3:40 p.m., an unsettling message from Taylor to another plane in his squadron was intercepted by Lieutenant Robert Cox, who was airborne over Fort Lauderdale on another exercise. "What is your trouble?" Cox asked Taylor. "Both my compasses are out and I am trying to find Fort Lauderdale," Taylor replied. For the next forty-five minutes, Cox tried to ascertain Taylor's position and direct him to land by orienting him toward the sun, but although it was a clear day, Taylor seemed unable to find it. Finally, Taylor's transmission faded until it stopped. Then, inexplicably, Cox's radio went dead, too. He returned to the field at Fort Lauderdale.

The ground station at Port Everglades had meanwhile established intermittent contact with the troubled Flight 19, confirming Cox's observations. Finally, at about a quarter past five, the ground station heard a forlorn message from Flight 19: "We'll fly west until we hit the beach or run out of gas."

The authorities at Fort Lauderdale ordered a search, and before long a Mariner flying boat was in the air with another thirteen crewmen. But the Mariner was not heard from again.

For the next five days, other search planes flew more than 930 sorties over the area, but not a scrap of wreckage from either the Avengers or the Mariner was ever recovered. Most analysts blame this and other disappearances that have occurred in the area on the normal hazards of the sea and air. But students of the occult blame the disaster on the malevolent powers said to flourish in the Bermuda Triangle.

A Leap across Space and Time

It was the "strange, cigar-shaped cloud," he recalled, that gave Bruce Gernon, Jr., the first hint that his flight on December 4, 1970, would be out of the ordinary. With his father as copilot, Gernon had just taken off in his Beechcraft Bonanza from Andros Island in the Bahamas, bound for Palm Beach, Florida.

Gernon remembers accelerating quickly to avoid the thick cloud, but it seemed to rise to meet him and then to envelop him. Spying a small tunnel through the cloud, he dived down, hoping to exit into clear sky on the other side. But this was no ordinary cloud. "The walls were glowing white with small white clouds rotating clockwise around the interior," Gernon later recalled. The plane seemed to pick up unnatural speed, and for several seconds, Gernon and his father experienced weightlessness. Then the airplane exited from the tunnel and entered a greenish white haze — not the blue sky he had seen ahead.

Trying to fix his position, Gernon was startled to observe his compass rotating counterclockwise. His navigational equipment would no longer function and he was unable to make contact with radar control.

Through the haze, he spotted an island and, calculating his flight time, thought it must be the Bimini keys. Minutes later, Gernon recognized it as Miami Beach instead. But how could that be? Little more than half the expected flight time had elapsed.

Landing at Palm Beach, Gernon checked his clock. A trip that normally took him about seventy-five minutes had taken only forty-five, and he had burned twelve fewer gallons of fuel than usual.

In the years that followed, Gernon considered himself among the lucky who lived to tell of an unaccountable journey through the Bermuda Triangle, having been the victim of an apparent time warp.

Richard Schlecht

45

CHAPTER 2

Secrets of the Great Pyramid

A fter a few days of scuba diving along the Red Sea coast of Egypt in early 1985, two French architects went on an excursion to see the Great Pyramid of Cheops at Giza. As they examined the huge structure, they noted a number of things that simply did not make sense to them. Some of the pyramid's immense stone blocks, for example, are stacked vertically, rather than staggered in their usual pattern. And in certain parts of the pyramid, curious roughhewn stones crop up in the midst of polished limestone.

Like generations of pyramid visitors before them, the two Frenchmen, Gilles Dormion and Jean-Patrice Goidin, were captivated by the great monument. And like so many others, they believed that they could penetrate its mysteries. The structural anomalies, the architects deduced, were clues to hidden, previously unknown rooms within the pyramid. They speculated that one such secret chamber might even contain the remains of the Pharaoh Cheops himself, thus resolving one of the pyramid's eternal questions: Where is the body it was presumably built to entomb?

Dormion and Goidin had considerable technological advantages over previous pyramid detectives. After several exploratory visits to the stone hallways, they returned in August of 1986 with a microgravimeter, a sophisticated instrument capable of registering density voids, or cavities, within the pyramid. And behind the walls of a corridor leading to the room known as the Queen's Chamber, the device detected the voids predicted by the architects. Encouraged, the two men got permission from Egyptian authorities to drill into the ancient limestone walls in search of the pyramid's secrets.

For days, the architects and their colleagues worked in the cramped passages of the pyramid, their drills chewing through more than two yards of rock in three different places. But all they uncovered were pockets of fine, crystalline sand: The microgravimeter, it seemed, could indicate the presence of voids in the pyramid but could not pinpoint their precise location. The secret chambers, if they exist, remained hidden. The Great Pyramid had thwarted yet another attempt in the long, frustrating, and fascinating quest to unravel its abiding riddles.

Since the time of the classical Greeks, people have gazed at this sole survivor of the ancient world's seven wonders and asked questions they could not answer. Why was it built? If it was a tomb, as conventional wisdom has generally supposed, why were no symbols or possessions of royalty—much less a royal corpse—ever found? If it was not a tomb, what was it? And how was it built? How, given the building techniques of the day, could one explain the astonishing precision of its construction, its near-perfect alignment to the points of the compass, the exquisite accuracy of its masonry? If the pyramid's design incorporates advanced mathematical and astronomical knowledge, as many investigators believe, how did its builders acquire such wisdom so far in advance of other civilizations? Could the enigmatic structure even harbor some sort of mystical powers beyond the realm of conventional science?

More than a few archeologists, astronomers, religious scholars, and amateur pyramid enthusiasts have argued such questions through the centuries. While archeologists focus on the structure purely as a historical artifact, other investigators have usually fallen into three schools of thought. The first, and most common, holds that the pyramid represents a universal system of measurement, that its very dimensions embody archetypal measures of length and even time. A splinter group of nineteenth-century pyramid students founded the second school, focusing on the structure's extraordinary properties as a gigantic sundial and an astronomical observatory. These so-called archeoastronomers made a strong case that the pyramid builders, whoever they were, had an awareness of astronomy and the earth's dimensions far superior to anything previously imagined.

As the fascination with the pyramid continued into the twentieth century, a third and far more speculative school arose, con-centrating on the pyramid shape itself and its alleged physical effects on both living things and inanimate objects. These researchers claimed that the pyramid shape could somehow help plants grow, keep food fresh longer, and even sharpen dull razor blades. Still others have accounted for the mathematical wisdom the structure supposedly embodies by imagining that its builders came from lost Atlantis, or even from another planet, or from both. The pyramid itself maintains a stubborn silence. It has never been completely explored nor completely explained.

The pyramid of Cheops rises in its enigmatic majesty from the rocky Giza plateau ten miles west of Cairo. Glimpsed through the branches of the acacia, eucalyptus, and tamarind trees that line the boulevard leading to the plateau, it vaults up from a wind-scraped flat on the edge of the Libyan Desert with dramatic suddenness, a breathtaking mountain of sand-colored stone looming above the lush palm groves of the nearby Nile. Caravan travelers approaching from the desert in ages past saw it for days before they reached it, a tiny triangle on the horizon bulking ever larger in its symmetrical perfection. Close up, its grandeur is overpowering. Numbers can only suggest its immensity—a ground area of 13.1 acres, the edifice itself composed of some 2.3 million limestone blocks averaging two and a half tons each. The structure contains enough stone to build a wall of foot-square cubes two-thirds of the way around the globe at the equator, a distance of 16,600 miles.

The Great Pyramid and the two others that stand near it on the plateau—attributed to Cheops's immediate successors—were erected during the period of Egyptian history known as the Fourth Dynasty, between 2613 and 2494 B.C. Egyptologists believe that Cheops (as the Greeks knew him; his Egyptian name was Khufu) ordered the immense building raised as a tomb and monument to himself. Its outer shell was originally composed of highly polished limestone blocks fitted together with painstaking precision, but these casing stones were stripped off in the fourteenth century and used in the construction of Cairo. At some point in history, the original capstone, forming the top thirty-one feet of the pyramid, was also removed.

Egyptologists have drawn on their knowledge of Egyptian religion to explain the significance of the pyramid shape, contending that it could have been connected with sun worship. The angled walls, they say, resemble the outspread rays of the sun descending earthward from a cloud, and the pyramid thus represents a stairway to the heavens. Some students of the ancient Egyptian Book of the Dead, such as the modern occultist writer Manly P. Hall, even maintain that the pyramid provided more than merely figurative passage to celestial realms. According to Hall, the building was a secret temple where the elect underwent a mystic ritual transforming them into gods. The initiates would lie for three days and nights within the pyramid while their *ka*—the soul or essence—left their bodies and entered "the spiritual spheres of space." In the process, the candidates "achieved actual immortality" and became godlike.

More down-to-earth questions surround the issue of how, in an age without pulleys or the wheel, the massive pyramid was built. But archeologists have guessed at a general scenario: The builders somehow leveled the site and then aligned the sides of the building by making repeated observations of circumpolar stars to determine true directions. At quarries a few miles away, masons cut the limestone with stone hammers and copper chisels. Crews consisting of hundreds of workers then dragged the blocks to the site; granite used in some parts of the interior was ferried down the Nile from a site about 400 miles distant and hauled up a causeway from the river. To pull the multiton blocks up the sides of the rising pyramid, they may have used a spiraling earthen ramp, although some experts believe they levered the stone upward on planks and wooden runners. The blocks were then fitted together with hairline precision, displaying an accuracy of engineering that impresses even present-day builders.

Many observers have doubted that so massive a structure as the Great Pyramid—a miracle of engineering, a prodigy of decades of backbreaking labor under the blazing sun—could have been intended merely for the housing of one royal mummy. Alternate explanations have flourished since the pre-Christian era. The Roman historian Julius Honorius declared that the pyramids were storehouses for grain. (Another early writer opined that the structures were extinct volcanoes.) The Arabs who ruled Egypt for centuries thought that they were repositories of ancient knowledge, built by earlier rulers who feared a catastrophe, perhaps the flood; local folktales claimed that the Great Pyramid incorporated both a guide to the stars and a prophecy of the future. Superstition trailed legend: Ghosts patrolled the corridors, the Arabs said, as did a naked woman with unsightly teeth who seduced trespassers and drove them mad.

The Greek historian Herodotus was the first visitor to gather and record information about the Great Pyramid in a systematic way. Herodotus visited Giza in the fifth century B.C., when the structure was already 2,000 years old, and wrote a description of its construction based on his conversations with local Egyptians. Unable to go inside the edifice (its entrance was hidden), he accepted his informants' claim that the pyramid was a tomb built to the tyrannical Khufu. The king's burial vault, they said, lay underground.

One hundred thousand men labored on the pyramid, according to Herodotus, with fresh crews thrown onto the project every three months. They built the causeway from the river to the plateau in ten years; the pyramid itself took another twenty years to complete. Engineers lifted the gigantic stones up the sides of the structure step by step using "machines formed of short wooden planks" on each step. Herodotus did not elaborate on how these machines worked. He was also told that outer casing stones were installed from the top down, after the interior core was in place. These glistening, highly polished stones were covered with inscriptions—later lost when the blocks were carted off to Cairo.

Herodotus was interested in the Great Pyramid primarily as an engineering project. But the next pyramid explorer known to history had a somewhat different perspective on the structure and introduced what was to become an abiding theme of pyramid studies: the quest for the mathematical wisdom possessed by the ancients.

The ninth-century Arab caliph Abdullah Al Mamun was a young ruler with a scientific turn of mind and a special interest in astronomy. He dreamed of mapping the world and charting the heavens, and he turned his attention to the pyramid when he learned that its secret chambers reportedly contained highly accurate maps and tables executed by the pyramid builders. In addition, and perhaps of more interest to the caliph's fellow explorers, great treasure was said to be hidden somewhere within.

Arab historians later told the dramatic tale of how the caliph and his team of architects, builders, and stonemasons set to work in A.D. 820. Unable to find an entrance to the inscrutable structure, they launched a frontal attack, heating the limestone blocks with fire and then dousing them with cold vinegar until they cracked. After burrowing through 100 feet of rock this way, the explorers finally reached a narrow, four-foot-high passageway that climbed steeply upward. At its upper end they found the pyramid's original entrance, forty-nine feet above the ground, blocked and hidden by a pivoting stone door. Turning around, the explorers followed the passageway downward. After crawling on their hands and knees through the inky darkness, they were chagrined to find only an unfinished, empty chamber. If secret writings or a king's ransom were to be found in the pyramid, it would be elsewhere.

Excitement was rekindled, however, when Al Mamun's men returned to the passageway and discovered what looked like another corridor sloping upward. Unfortunately, its entrance was completely filled by a large granite plug, obviously placed there deliberately. The granite was impervious to their hammers and chisels, but the determined Arabs found that they could chip through the softer limestone blocks around it. As soon as they did, though, they found another granite obstacle and then several more. Someone had been determined to bar intruders from the pyramid's inner sanctum.

After laboriously hacking their way around the series of plugs, the explorers emerged into a low-ceilinged corridor that slanted upward until it intersected a level passageway. This led them to an eighteen-foot-square, twenty-foot-high gabled room that would later become known as the Queen's Chamber (because of the Arab custom of burying women in tombs with gabled roofs). No queen was in evidence, however; this chamber, too, was empty.

The weary Arabs returned to the ascending passageway and found that it expanded abruptly into a splendid corridor, whose walls of polished limestone, twenty-eight feet high, later earned it the name of Grand Gallery. Still sloping upward, the gallery climbed 156 feet more before it gave onto an antechamber; beyond that was the largest room in the interior, an imposing sanctum thirty-four feet long, seventeen feet wide, and nineteen feet high, later called the King's Chamber.

Al Mamun and his men stepped gingerly across the threshold, doubtless convinced that this was the fabulous prize for which they had all worked so hard. And there, against a red granite wall, they saw it—a large, chocolate-colored stone sarcophagus, so big that the chamber must have been built around it. Thrusting their torches ahead of them, the explorers rushed to look inside. They found nothing. The granite sarcophagus was empty.

In a frenzy of disappointment, the Arabs ripped up part of the floor and hacked at the walls, hoping to find some trace of treasure. Al Mamun could only conclude that either the empty sarcophagus was all that was ever there or that looters had long ago pillaged the room. But if earlier marauders had indeed made their way to the chamber, a basic question remained unanswered: How did they get by the stone plugs that had stymied the caliph and his men?

Eight hundred years passed before the next stride in pursuit of pyramid learning. During this time, Europe had emerged from the Dark Ages into a luminous era of expansion and exploration. Adventurers, merchants, and statesmen alike were hampered, however, by their ignorance of world geography and by the lack of a single internationally accepted unit of weight, length, and geographical degree. In response, scholars turned—as they so often did—to the ancients, hoping to find some forgotten, fundamental unit of measure based on precise knowledge of the earth's dimensions.

In search of this knowledge, British mathematician John Greaves visited Egypt in 1638. The bookish thirty-six-year-old had spent most of his life within the confines of academia, first at Oxford and then as a professor of geometry at Gresham

An Occultist's Honeymoon

A number of overnight visitors to the Great Pyramid have reported odd happenings within its walls, but the strangest experience by far was related by Aleister Crowley, self-styled "Great Beast" of the occult world.

Crowley was an Englishman who had founded a secret society devoted to what he called sexual magic. He visited the pyramid on his honeymoon in 1903, declaring his intention to spend a night in the King's Chamber. Once ensconced there with his bride, he lit a candle and began to read an incantation. All at once, Crowley later reported, a pale lilac light bathed the room, allowing him to continue without his candle.

Despite this mystic illumination, Crowley had a rather prosaic complaint about his bridal suite. The hard stone floor, he said, made sleep impossible.

Mrs. Crowley's opinion is not recorded.

51

The eternal allure of the pyramids is evident in this nineteenth-century painting of dawn on the Giza platea

The largest structure is the Great Pyramid of Cheops; its neighbors are monuments to that pharaoh's successors.

College in London. But books, Greaves found, were no substitute for experience. He traveled first to Italy, where he measured Roman monuments to find the legendary Roman foot (a fraction of an inch shorter than the British foot, he concluded), and then to Giza.

Greaves believed, as had the ninth-century Arab caliph Al Mamun before him, that the pyramid builders had possessed a geometrical wisdom now lost to the world. Hoping to discover the unit of measurement they had employed, Greaves mounted the thirty-eight-foot-high pile of debris around the pyramid's base, instruments in hand, and clambered through Al Mamun's makeshift entrance.

The first thing he encountered was a blizzard of bats; these he dispersed by firing his pistol. He then scrambled around the granite plugs as the Arabs had done, meticulously measured the King's Chamber and the sarcophagus (6.488 feet long, which suggested to Greaves that human dimensions had not changed) and marveled at the precise masonry. His main find, however, was a narrow well, which plunged straight down into darkness from the bottom of the Grand Gallery. Was it an escape route for the builders after they lodged the stone plugs in place? a getaway passage for looters? Greaves never found out; the bats and foul air forced

him to give up a reconnaissance descent after only sixty feet. Greaves finished his studies of the pyramid by measuring the structure's height and base, figuring the first at 481 feet and the second at 693 feet per side; the latter estimate turned out to be short of the mark. He then returned home to present his data in a booklet eruditely entitled *Pyramidographia*.

The mathematician had not found the basic unit of measure he sought, but his booklet, containing his measurements and description of the pyramid, reached some of the greatest minds of the day. For example, William Harvey, discoverer of the circulation of blood, correctly deduced that Greaves had overlooked a system of ventilation within the pyramid (discovered by later explorers); physicist Sir Isaac Newton used Greaves's figures to derive measurements he called sacred and profane cubits. Newton hoped these basic units would help him determine the circumference of the earth, a figure essential to his theory of gravitation. Unfortunately, Greaves's numbers were not accurate enough for this purpose, and Newton had to wait a few years until scientists established the length of a geographical degree.

The next assault on the pyramids was a literal one. In July of 1798, disciplined French troops commanded by General

The inside of the first and fairest Pyramid

If you imagine the whole Pyramid to be divided in the midst of a plane extended from the North side to the South: the entrance Galleries, and Chambers, with the several passages to them, will appeare in this manner

AB the entrance into the Pyramid
BC the ascent into the First Galery
CE the first Gallery
DR the Well
GH the passage in the arched Chamber
HI the arched Chamber
FK the second Gallery
KNQ the first anticloset
NQO the second anticloset
OP the Chamber in which the tombe stands

A cross-section from John Greaves's book
Pyramidographia depicts the passages, chambers, and galleries of
the Great Pyramid, as measured in 1638.

54

Napoleon Bonaparte routed scimitar-wielding Egyptians at the bloody Battle of the Pyramids. And it was not very long afterward that the young Bonaparte began to attack the secrets of the Great Pyramid on the Giza plateau with a corps of French scientists—savants, they were called—who were attached to his army. The savants were intrigued by many of the same questions about the pyramid and its builders that had teased John Greaves more than a century and a half before. Principal among the pyramid students was a young scientist named Edmé-François Jomard, who had studied the slender archive of pyramid literature, much of it unreliable, that had accumulated over the centuries. Like Greaves, he was especially eager to establish the unit of measurement that the builders used and to discover whether those measures were derived from the dimensions of the earth—as was the metric system, recently adopted by revolutionary France. (The meter was then defined as 1/10,000,000 of the quadrant of the earth's circumference from the North Pole to the equator.)

Jomard and his colleagues quickly abandoned their attempt to investigate the pyramid's interior when they encountered the formidable mounds of guano deposited by the resident bats. The indignant animals, a chastened French colonel reported, "scratched with their claws and stifled with the acrid stench of their bodies." Driven back, the savants turned to the structure's exterior. Aided by a work force of 150 Turks, they cleared tons of sand and debris from the northwest and northeast corners and discovered two rectangular depressions in the base rock where the original cornerstones, carried off centuries earlier, had rested. This gave them two good anchors for a measurement of the pyramid's base, although their work was still hampered by piles of debris along the north wall.

First Jomard measured one side of the base: 230.9 meters, or 757.5 feet. Then he struggled along to the thirty-three-square-foot platform at the summit of the truncated edifice, tried unsuccessfully to slingshot a stone beyond the base, and patiently measured the height of each stone step on his descent: total elevation, 146.6 meters, or 481 feet. With these figures Jomard calculated the angle of the slope of the pyramid as fifty-one degrees nineteen minutes, and its apothem—the line from the apex to the midpoint of each of its four sides at the bottom—was measured as 184.7 meters, or 606 feet.

The young scientist knew that early writers had described the pyramid's apothem as one stadium long. He also remembered that the length of a stadium, a basic unit of measurement in the ancient world, was believed to be related to the circumference of the earth. His figure for the apothem was thus a number to conjure with. Jomard turned his attention next to the cubit, another ancient measure of length. Herodotus had written that a stadium contained 400 cubits, so the Frenchman divided his figure for the apothem by 400, which gave him a cubit measure of .4618 meters. Other Greek authorities on the subject had declared the base of the Great Pyramid to be 500 cubits long. When Jomard multiplied his .4618 by 500, the result was 230.9 meters, exactly what he had totaled up for the base length.

To Jomard the message was clear: The Egyptians had an

The Voice of the Sphinx

Towering sixty-six feet above the swirling sands of the Giza plateau, the Great Sphinx has for millennia proved as fascinating as it is majestic. For many, the impassive face and knowing smile have come to embody the lost wisdom of the ancient world.

This most inscrutable of structures appears to have been built of stone from the depleted quarry already used for the Giza pyramids: In about 2700 B.C., stoneworkers cut out the best and hardest rock for the Great Pyramid and its neighbors, shunning the softer bedrock. Masons then transformed these leavings into the Great Sphinx, sculpting its massive head with an

After excavating the Sphinx, Thutmose IV commemorated his dream with a granite tablet.

idealized likeness of Pharaoh Chephren, complete with royal headdress.

Through the centuries, sandstorms have threatened to engulf the Sphinx, giving rise to one of its most enduring stories: Around 1400 B.C., when the Sphinx was buried up to its neck, a prince on a hunt stopped to rest in the shadow of the figure's head and soon fell asleep. In a dream, he heard the voice of the Sphinx promise to make him ruler of Egypt ahead of his older brothers if he would clear away the sand. On awakening, the prince vowed to keep his part of the bargain. He completed the task shortly after ascending to the throne as Pharaoh Thutmose IV.

Legend claims that when the Sphinx was buried in sand, visitors would seek wisdom from its lips.

advanced knowledge of geometry. They knew the size of the earth, they derived their units of measure from the earth's circumference, and they built this knowledge into the Great Pyramid. The evidence was in the stones.

Unfortunately for Jomard, measurements made with inexact instruments amid the migrating sands of the desert could be tantalizingly inexact. The task of pyramid measuring was greatly complicated by the wind-blown sand and debris that gathered in huge mounds all around the structure; investigators had to engage in heavy-duty excavation work just to get next to the base to measure it. It was thus no surprise that Jomard's colleagues, upon remeasuring the base and height, came up with slightly different results. Furthermore, they pointed out, no evidence of Jomard's cubit could be found in other ancient Egyptian structures.

In the end, the French savants refused to abandon their belief that it was the Greeks, not the Egyptians, who founded the science of geometry. When they returned home and published an elaborate, twenty-four-volume report on their findings (which included the Rosetta Stone, the key to Egyptian hieroglyphics), Jomard's stubbornly maintained argument was given short shrift.

The French scientific safari and the subsequent accounts of it that began appearing in Europe inspired an explosion of interest in things Egyptian. Nineteenth-century Europeans fell in love with Egypt: Museums vied for mummies, statues, and obelisks; artists grafted pyramids into sylvan landscapes; Empire and Regency fashion designers borrowed Egyptian motifs, and aristocrats had sphinxes and crocodiles carved onto their furniture. The Scottish peer Alexander, tenth duke of Hamilton, even had himself mummified. Americans succumbed to the craze as well: The city of Memphis, Tennessee, took its name from an older river city in Egypt. In 1880, New Yorkers imported an obelisk called Cleopatra's Needle and installed it in Central Park.

Pyramid themes became fashionable just as society, particularly the society of Victorian England, was entering a troubling time, an era in which modern science seemed to threaten traditional religious beliefs. In response, some religiously oriented scholars seized upon the mysterious structures as proof of the divine hand's presence in the world.

The first major proponent of this theory was a London editor and critic named John Taylor. Taylor was a widely educated and deeply religious man: He was as well versed in the Scriptures as he was in mathematics, astronomy, and literature. After starting out as an apprentice to a bookseller, Taylor had risen by the 1820s to the post of editor of *London Magazine;* his distinguished circle of acquaintances included poets John Clare and John Keats. Nevertheless, he "frightened away half his friends," according to one of them, with what was to become a thirty-year-long obsession with the mystery of the Great Pyramid.

Taylor never visited Egypt; instead, he built a scale model of the pyramid to aid his studies. Dismissing the tomb hypothesis, Taylor pored over the figures gathered by Jomard and others in search of unifying principles. He found to his surprise that when he divided the perimeter of the pyramid by twice its height, the result was a number nearly identical to the value of pi (3.14159+), the constant that is multiplied by the diameter of a circle to give its circumference. To Taylor, this was a tantalizing discovery: If the pyramid builders were aware of pi, which was not known to have been correctly calculated to the fourth decimal point until the sixth century, what else did they know? For one thing, he concluded, they knew the circumference of the globe; for another, the distance from the center of the earth to the poles.

With pi as the connecting link, Taylor determined that the ratio of the pyramid's altitude to its perimeter was the same as that of the polar radius of the earth to its circumference: 2π. Far from being a mere burial vault, Taylor decided, the pyramid was a structural expression of the wisdom of the ancients. "It was to make a record of the measure of the earth that it was built," he declared.

But Taylor doubted that Egyptian scholars of the Fourth Dynasty had themselves possessed the knowledge built into the pyramid. Such wisdom had to come from God. "It is probable," he wrote, "that to some human beings in the earliest ages of society, a degree of intellectual power was given by the Creator, which raised them far above the level of those succeeding inhabitants of the earth." God instructed the pyramid builders just as he had directed Noah to build the ark, according to Taylor, who also believed that humanity had been sliding downhill intellectually ever since.

Taylor was seventy-eight years old when his book, *The Great Pyramid: Why Was It Built? And Who Built It?*, appeared in 1859. While Taylor's sweeping theories were well received in some circles, the Royal Society politely declined to hear a paper he wrote on the subject. But before his death a few years later, he had made at least one influential convert— Charles Piazzi Smyth, Astronomer-Royal of Scotland.

Smyth's social and intellectual credentials equaled Taylor's: He was the son of an admiral and the godson of renowned Italian astronomer Giuseppe Piazzi, discoverer of the first known asteroid. Smyth's own accomplishments in astronomy had won him the Scottish post at the tender age of twenty-six; twelve years later, an important paper presented on optics gained him election to Edinburgh's Royal Society, a coveted honor for any scientist. Yet pyramidology, hardly a popular subject with the Royal Society just then, came to dominate his professional career.

Captivated by Taylor, Smyth warmed to the dying editor's cause with an ardor that, like Taylor's, was in equal parts scientific and religious, with a dash of patriotism thrown in. His reading persuaded him that the basic unit of measurement was what he called the pyramid inch, a distance he identified as 1/25th of a cubit and within a thousandth part of a British inch. This was timely ammunition in the campaign by British scientists against the adoption of the metric system devised by the French, a proposal that Smyth viewed with nationalistic alarm.

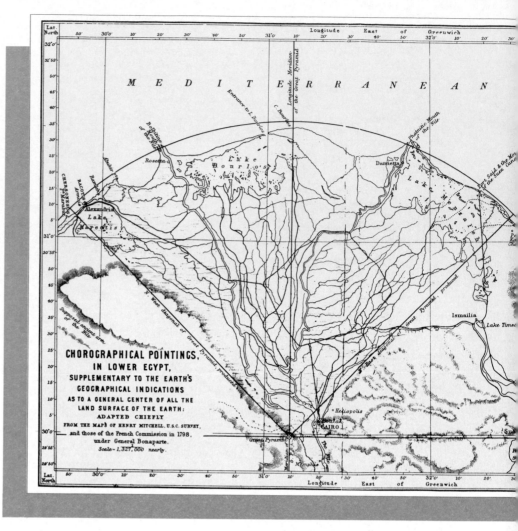

In late 1864, the forty-five-year-old astronomer left for Egypt with his wife to do what Taylor had not done—make his own survey and measurements. Armed with trunks of up-to-date instruments, including a camera, the Smyths set up camp in an abandoned cliffside tomb where they could recline on campstools and watch clouds of bats billow out of the pyramid at dusk. Smyth spent several nights on the pyramid's summit, making astronomic observations showing that the pyramid was sited within minutes of latitude thirty degrees north. Smyth also observed that the pyramid's shadow disappeared completely at the spring equinox and concluded that this indicated advanced knowledge of astronomy. His measurements of the external dimensions yielded figures that matched pi even more closely than Taylor's had, to the fifth digit beyond the decimal point.

Smyth was in agreement with Taylor's opinion that the Great Pyramid enshrined the ancients' scientific knowledge. Its built-in measures were "more admirably and learnedly earth-commensurable," he wrote, "than anything which has ever entered into the mind of man to conceive." Smyth even went beyond Taylor to claim that measures of time as well as

Maps of the Giza plateau suggest the role of extraordinary
geographical knowledge in the Great Pyramid's construction.
Below, a plan of the plateau shows the exact north-south
alignment of the pyramids, while, at left, an expanded view reveals
that the structure stands at the apex of the Nile Delta.

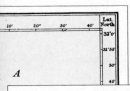

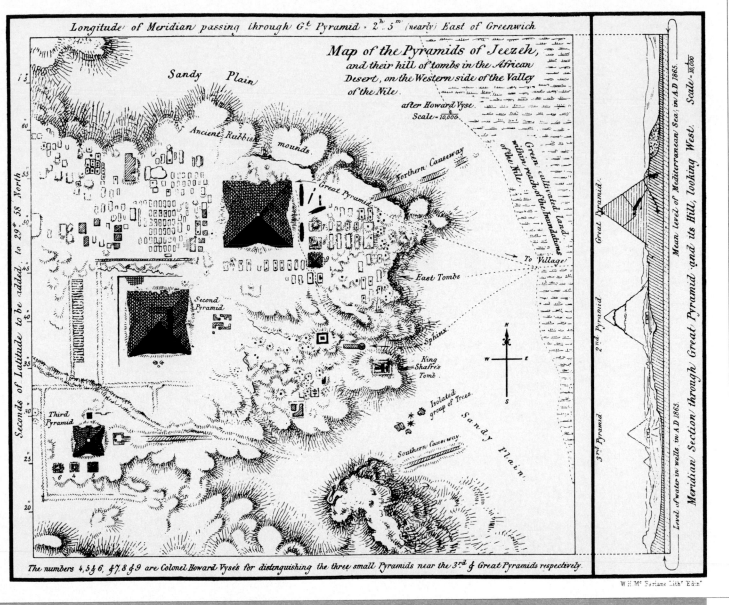

Longitude of Meridian passing through G.ʰ Pyramid - 2ʰ. 5ᵐ (nearly) East of Greenwich

Map of the Pyramids of Jeezeh,
and their hill of tombs in the African
Desert, on the Western side of the Valley
of the Nile.

after Howard Vyse.
Scale = 10,000

The numbers 4, 5 & 6, & 7, 8 & 9 are Colonel Howard Vyse's for distinguishing the three small Pyramids near the 3.ʳᵈ & Great Pyramids respectively.

W. H. Mᶜ Farlane Lith.ʳ Edin.ʳ

of distance were incorporated into the building of the pyramid. According to the astronomer, the structure's perimeter, in pyramid inches, equaled precisely 1,000 times 365.2, the number of days in a solar year. The builders had worked all of this out with their breathtaking gift for physics, Smyth wrote, 1500 years before "the infantine beginning of such things among the ancient Greeks."

In his subsequent book *Our Inheritance in the Great Pyramid*, Smyth concluded, as had Taylor before him, that only God could have engineered the Great Pyramid. The Bible, he said, states that in ages past God imparted "wisdom, and metrical instructions for buildings" to a chosen few "for some special and unknown purpose." In later years, Smyth argued that the pyramid also revealed the distance from the earth to the sun when its height in inches was multiplied by ten to the ninth power; ten to nine being the proportion of height to width of the pyramid. In addition, the structure not only proved the existence of God but also predicted the date of the second coming of Christ.

Although Smyth's colorful writing style helped sell his

An Obelisk's Perilous Voyage

Egypt's stone obelisks — originally raised in homage to the sun-gods — have been coveted since Roman times as symbols of conquest and mysterious power. Weighing an average of 150 tons, the granite pillars challenged those who would carry them off, as Sir James Alexander discovered in 1877.

The obelisk of the Englishman's attentions was Cleopatra's Needle, sixty-eight feet tall. It had been presented to England half a century earlier by the Egyptian ruler Mohammed Ali. Attempts to collect the prize in Alexandria, however, had met only with frustration. Bringing it home was a matter of pride for the patriotic Alexander. His solution was to encase the obelisk in a watertight iron cylinder and roll it to the sea on huge timber wheels *(right)*. Once afloat, the cylinder was fitted out with a keel, rudder, deck, and cabin.

Appropriately christened the *Cleopatra,* this strange vessel was hauled out to sea by the steamship *Olga* on September 21, 1877. The journey was a harrowing one, marked by a gale that forced the captain temporarily to abandon his foundering ship. Reclaimed and repaired, the monument glided into the Thames River on January 21, 1878, and was installed on the river's banks. The obelisk remains there to this day, still invoking Egyptian sun-gods under London's rainy skies.

Cleopatra's Needle (left) is one of a matching pair. Its twin stands in New York's Central Park.

An 1877 newspaper (right) reports the abandonment of the Cleopatra. The obelisk was feared lost, but the ship's captain brought it home in 1878.

THE ILLUSTRATED
LONDON NEWS

books, he failed to win over many of his scientific colleagues. Egyptologists denounced him, and a fellow member of the Royal Society of Edinburgh called his ideas "strange hallucinations which only a few weak women believe." A critic from the United States drolly expressed the skeptics' view that numbers could be marshaled to prove almost anything: "If a suitable unit of measurement is found," he said, "an exact equivalent to the distance to Timbuktu is certain to be found . . . in the number of street lamps in Bond Street, or the specific gravity of mud, or the mean weight of adult goldfish."

Even so, the work of Taylor and Smyth bred many disciples, who found that the more they investigated the Great Pyramid, the more hidden spiritual, scientific, and historical messages they uncovered. American churchman Joseph Seiss wrote in 1877 that its stones harbored "one great system of interrelated numbers, measures, weights, angles, temperatures, degrees, geometric problems and cosmic references." Seiss was particularly struck by the pyramid's unrelenting fiveness: It had five corners and five sides (including the base), and a pyramid inch was one-fifth of one-fifth of a cubit. Was it only coincidental, he asked, that we have five senses, five fingers or toes per limb, and that there are five books of Moses?

Pyramidologists also pointed to an extraordinary fact: The latitude and longitude lines that intersect at the pyramid — thirty degrees north and thirty-one degrees east — cross more dry land than any others. Was it possible that the ancient Egyptians had known this and sited their immense structure at the very center of the habitable world? On a smaller scale, a quadrant extending in straight lines northwest and northeast from the pyramid neatly encompasses the entire Nile Delta (*page 58*). Ancient surveyors might have found this useful in a land whose boundaries were regularly flooded.

It was the pyramid's purported religious significance, however, that sparked the most heated debates in Victorian England. The pyramidologists' contention that the structure was divinely inspired intensified the clash between the evolutionists, newly armed with Charles Darwin's radical ideas about the origins of life, and Christian fundamentalists who believed in the Bible's literal truth. Smyth and his followers, totaling up the pyramid inches, viewed the pyramid as immutable evidence of a divinity who created the world in 4004 B.C.—the year computed by the seventeenth-century Irish churchman James Usher and widely accepted by the orthodox. The human being's remotest ancestors, therefore, were not forest-dwelling primates but master builders doing God's bidding. In the United States, a group banded together to advocate a system of measures based on sacred pyramid cubits, in opposition to the atheistic metric system; President James Garfield was a member of the organization.

Clearly, the pyramid controversy required the illumination of pure science, unencumbered by preconceptions or wishful thinking. And in 1880, a twenty-six-year-old Englishman with the ponderous name of William Matthew Flinders Petrie set out for Egypt with an array of sophisticated instruments, hoping to resolve all speculation about the structure's dimensions and alignment.

Flinders Petrie, as he was called, was well qualified by pedigree and training for such a task. His maternal grandfather and namesake, Captain Matthew Flinders, was known for his explorations of Australia. His father, William Petrie, was an engineer who had been so struck by the writings of Taylor and Smyth that he became a dedicated pyramidologist himself, spending twenty years in the design and fabrication of special surveying equipment that would measure the Great Pyramid with unprecedented precision. Following his father's lead, the young Flinders Petrie read Smyth's book at the age of thirteen. Enchanted by the notion of varying standards of measure, Petrie took up the surveyor's trade and devoted himself to touring through England and painstakingly recording the dimensions of various buildings and ancient megalithic sites such as the great stone circles of Stonehenge.

When he arrived at the Giza plateau with his ample store of provisions and the crates bearing his father's carefully crafted instruments, Petrie did as so many other pyramid explorers had done before him and took up temporary residence in an empty cliffside tomb. Then he went to work, meticulously measuring and remeasuring every conceivable dimension of the Great Pyramid and its two smaller neighbors. To keep curious—and bothersome—British sightseers at bay, he sometimes went about his outdoor tasks clad only in vest and pants, both a shocking pink. In the hot, dusty interior of the pyramid, he often worked nude and late at night, after the irksome tourists had departed. The work was not without its hazards, as a friend, a certain Dr. Grant, found when he joined the surveyor one night. "I had a terrifying time when he fainted in the well," wrote Petrie. "To raise a very heavy man, barely conscious, up a shaft of seventy feet with scanty foothold, when at any moment he might sweep me away down to the bottom, was a risk not to be forgotten."

Petrie was astounded by the precision of the pyramid's stonework. Using instruments that were accurate to a tenth of an inch, he reported that the errors in the edifice both in length and in angles were so slight that a thumb would cover them. The walls of the descending passageway were within a quarter inch of being perfectly straight for their 350-foot length. He compared the joining of the casing stones to "the finest opticians' work on a scale of acres." The quality began to deteriorate, however, in the anteroom of the King's Chamber, leading the youthful surveyor to speculate that the original architect had not finished the job.

The results of Petrie's labors, published in an 1883 book entitled *The Pyramids and Temples of Gizeh,* were both gratifying and mortifying for Smyth and the pyramidologists. Petrie confirmed the pi relationship between the pyramid's height and perimeter. He found that the King's Chamber also incorporated pi in the ratio of its length to its periphery. But his figure for the pyramid's base was shorter than Smyth's, thus refuting the Scot's theory that the base length reflected the number of days in a year. Petrie also arrived at a different cubit measure, and he found no evidence to support Smyth's cherished pyramid inch.

Having located what he called "the ugly little fact which killed the beautiful theory," Petrie went on to an illustrious career in Egyptology, which eventually earned him a knighthood. And his data on the pyramid's dimensions remained the best available until a definitive 1925 survey by the Egyptian government ended the numerical arguments for good. It turned out that the four sides varied in length by no more than eight inches: The south side was 756.1 feet long, the east 755.9, the west 755.8, and the north 755.4. Even more impressive, the sides were almost perfectly aligned to the cardinal points of the compass. The French savant Jomard had estimated the height correctly at 481 feet, but he had miscalculated the angle of the sides, which is fifty-one degrees fifty-two minutes.

But even after Petrie effectively dismantled it, the pyramidologists' theory refused to die, and new discoveries continued to surface throughout the twentieth century. British engineer David Davidson, who began as a scornful agnostic and twenty-five years later became a true believer, managed to reconcile Petrie's findings with Smyth's through a complex set of calculations that factored in the virtually invisible hollowing of the pyramid's walls—which are in fact not completely flat but very slightly concave. Petrie had taken this into account, Davidson said, but had not extended his computations to the original outer casing. When this was done, according to Davidson, Smyth turned out to be right about the perimeter representing the solar year. In 1924, Davidson the erstwhile doubter wound up publishing a dense, 568-page book that concluded that the pyramid was "truth in structural form."

The measurement school would continue to arouse accusations of number juggling among the scientific establishment. The modern skeptical author Martin Gardner, for example, has poked sly fun at the fiveness obsession of Joseph Seiss by applying the same criteria to America's Washington Monument. Not only, says Gardner, is its height 555 feet five inches, but its base is fifty-five feet square and its windows are 500 feet from the base. Gardner's so-called monument foot yields a base of 56.5 feet, which when multiplied by the capstone weight gives a number very close to the speed of light. Could this be coincidence? asks Gardner.

The pyramid's dimensions have not been the only subject of scrutiny, however. At the same time that Petrie and Davidson were counting cubits, other British scholars were looking to the skies. In the late nineteenth century, British

The Cursed Treasures of Tut

Few treasures and no kingly remains have been found in the pyramids. But the discovery made by Egyptologist Howard Carter has served as a reminder — and, perhaps, a warning — of what could be in these monuments.

In November of 1922, after fifteen years of digging in the Valley of Kings south of Cairo, Carter and his financial backer, George Edward Herbert, fifth earl of Carnarvon, broke through the sealed entryway to a sunken tomb. There they discovered a magnificent collection of vases, chariots, thrones, and jewels. This, they knew, was the resting place of Pharaoh Tutankhamen, familiarly known as Tut.

Yet apprehension attended their triumph. Rumor had it that hieroglyphics warned of vengeance on intruders. A cobra — the symbol of Egyptian royalty — had devoured a canary belonging to Carter. To some, the meaning was clear: A terrible punishment would befall those who violated Tut's tomb.

Undaunted, the expeditioners spent the next year excavating before opening the chamber containing Tut's sarcophagus. But Lord Carnarvon did not live to see it. He had died of blood poisoning months earlier — the victim, some said, of a pharaoh's curse.

As his assistants look on, archeologist Howard Carter carefully opens a set of nested doors leading to the long-hidden sarcophagus of Tutankhamen.

astronomer Richard Proctor pioneered the approach to pyramid studies that would come to be called archeoastronomy. Proctor's research findings showed that before it was completed, the Great Pyramid might have been used as an astronomical observatory, as both Arab historians and the Roman writer Proclus had maintained.

The British astronomer argued that the perfect north-south alignment of the interior passages, together with their twenty-six-degree angle, enabled the Egyptians to use them as the equivalent of a telescope. By sighting celestial phenomena through the opening at the end of the passageway, ancient stargazers might have mapped the northern heavens. Those stationed in the Pyramid's Grand Gallery—he called them "watchmen of the night"—could have charted the transit of the principal stars across an arc of about eighty degrees. When the passages were ultimately sealed off, however, these watchmen would have lost their vantage points.

Egyptologists retorted that Egyptian science was not that advanced, but Proctor's thesis received considerable support when eminent British astronomer Sir J. Norman Lockyer published his book about pyramids and the stars, *The Dawn of Astronomy,* in 1894. Lockyer was not a man to be ignored. Discoverer of helium, a fellow of the Royal Society, and a scholar knighted by Queen Victoria for his accomplishments, Lockyer toured ancient Egyptian buildings and discovered that they were oriented toward the rising and setting of the sun and certain major stars at particular times of the year. Later, he made similar findings about the British megaliths at Stonehenge. Livio Stecchini, an American professor of the history of science and an expert on ancient measurement, would later contend that the Egyptians' meticulous astronomical observations enabled them to calculate the length of a degree of latitude and longitude to within a few hundred feet, an achievement that was not equaled until 4,000 years later, in the eighteenth century A.D.

The quest to decode the pyramid would continue into the late twentieth century, contributing to an ever-increasing body of pyramid theory, pyramid speculation, and pyramid lore. The most intriguing—and frequently derided—notion to flower in recent decades has focused not on the Great Pyramid itself but on the pyramid shape. According to some theorists, a factor inherent in that shape, something not clearly understood, seems to exert a force that has peculiar effects on objects, plants, and even people. This idea, which came to be known as pyramid power, derives primarily from a series of observations and experiments reported since the 1920s. Its first manifestation occurred in 1859, however, at the seat of mystery itself, the great mountain of stone at Giza.

Werner von Siemens, founder of the giant German electrical company that bears his name, had stopped at Giza in that year while shepherding a crew of engineers to the Red Sea, where they were to lay a telegraph cable. Ever curious and venturesome, Siemens set out to scramble to the summit of the pyramid; as he labored up the sides, the desert wind raised a pale mist of sand around him. Reaching the top, Siemens struck a victorious pose and jabbed a finger into the air. At that, a prickling sensation ran through his finger and a sharp noise rang out. The effect was similar to a mild electric shock.

Siemens, who knew a thing or two about the infant science of electricity, decided to conduct a test. Wrapping wet paper around a metal-necked wine bottle, he improvised a Leyden jar, a simple device for storing static electricity. When he held this contrivance above his head, Siemens was gratified to discover that the bottle became electrically charged, generating sparks when touched.

In itself, Siemens's electrical experience may not be particularly noteworthy. Under certain atmospheric conditions, others have noticed similar effects atop tall, pointed buildings. But it is more difficult to match the even stranger phenomenon reported in the early 1930s by a French ironmonger named Antoine Bovis. According to Bovis, he had been touring the King's Chamber in about 1920 when he came across the remains of several cats and other small animals that apparently had died in the pyramid. Curiously, the bodies had no odor. When he examined them, Bovis found that the animals had dehydrated and mummified despite the chamber's humidity.

Back home in Nice, the Frenchman determined to learn

about this oddity. After building a wooden model of the pyramid, he oriented it due north and placed a recently deceased cat inside. The body mummified in a few days. Bovis repeated the experiment with other dead animals as well as with meat and eggs; in every case, he claimed, the organic matter dried out and mummified instead of decaying.

Even more mystifying was the next revelation. Czech radio engineer Karl Drbal, having heard of Bovis's experiments, repeated them, using a cardboard pyramid to mummify beef and flowers. He then placed a razor blade inside his six-inch model, at a point a third of the way from the bottom (corresponding to the location of the King's Chamber). Drbal expected the blade to lose its edge. To his amazement, he said, it emerged sharper than before. He claimed that in subsequent tests the pyramid shape regenerated blades so that they could be used as many as 200 times.

Drbal speculated that this was produced by an unknown energy that affected the crystals in the blades. Others might have observed that such single-blade marathons have been achieved without mystic sharpening. In May 1926, for example, a Viennese named Oskar Jähnisch informed the Gillette Safety Razor Company that he had completed five years of daily shaving with a single Gillette blade. But after a ten-year delay, an initially skeptical Czech patent office issued a patent to Drbal in 1959 for the cardboard (later plastic) pyramids he called Cheops Pyramid Razor Blade Sharpeners.

The forces attributed to the pyramid shape continued to multiply. According to the pyramid power school of thought, people can enjoy the benign influences of pyramid energy directly by purchasing a vinyl pyramid tent and crawling inside. Asserted therapeutic effects include calmer children, diminished menstrual cramps, sharpened mental acuity, improved sleep, and an increased sex drive. A dentist in California suspended seventy-two little metal pyramids over his patients' chair. The result, he said, was less pain and quicker healing.

G. Patrick Flanagan of Glendale, California, a leading promoter of pyramid power, claimed that a form of energy dubbed biocosmic exists in pyramid-shaped objects. He described it grandly as "the very essence of the life force itself." Flanagan's research subjects included alfalfa sprouts and his pet poodle: The sprouts grew faster in a model pyramid and the dog, after sleeping inside one for several weeks, became a vegetarian. Like Drbal, Flanagan decided to go into the pyramid business, marketing both tents and energy plates, made of several tiny pyramids fused together, which he maintained would energize anything placed on them.

The pyramid power idea did not fare well among most scientists, however. Stanford Research Institute experiments at the Great Pyramid showed that food stored inside deteriorated normally. Geologist Charles Cazeau and anthropologist Stuart Scott conducted research of their own, reporting with amusement that "eggs . . . came out of our pyramid after 43 days a smelly, runny yellow, and full of sediment. . . . Tomatoes in pyramids fared no better than those in brown paper bags. We were unable to sharpen razor blades."

Researchers continue to pursue the enduring questions about the Great Pyramid itself, the who and how and why that have perplexed travelers to Giza for more than two millennia. In the mid-1980s, Egyptologists designed the first highly detailed map of the Giza plateau in an effort to learn more about the pyramid's construction. Using sophisticated theodolites—instruments that measure angles—and aerial photographs, archeologist Mark Lehner and his crew detected nearby quarries and deduced a method by which the ancient builders might have created the pyramid's amazingly level base: Trenches cut into the rock could have been filled with water; wooden surveying stakes would then have been inserted into the water and marked against its naturally level surface.

Other theorists have sought to explain how the Egyptians could have cut stone so precisely and hauled it so far. French chemist Joseph Davidovits went a step further, claiming in 1974 that they were chemists rather than stonemasons. Basing his conclusion on analysis of pyramid rock samples, Davidovits maintained that the huge blocks were cast, not cut. In the Davidovits scenario, a puttylike substance was formed on the site from available liquids and minerals. This mixture was then poured into a mold and fired under low heat until it resembled granite. Davidovits produced such stones in his laboratory, but he has not yet convinced archeologists that the Egyptians did the same on the Giza sands.

Pyramidologists still voice familiar, sweeping themes of prophecy and revelation. Writer Max Toth has proclaimed that only the discovery of a secret room stands between twentieth-century man and the "Masters of the Mysteries," who are silently waiting to "reclothe him in the vestments of truth."

Other visionaries have seen the pyramid as the missing link between recorded history and Atlantis. Manly P. Hall, an enthusiastic student of ancient religions, has proposed that the most gifted scientists in the highly developed civilization of Atlantis, aware that disaster was imminent, fled to Egypt and built the pyramid as a repository for both their learning and their treasure. By concealing their wisdom in the pyramid, Hall suggested, the advanced Atlanteans made certain that only those who were worthy would discover and understand it.

However fanciful Hall's thesis may be, the pyramid's secrets are elusive, despite the best efforts of traditional scientists and the far-from-traditional pyramidologists. Whatever we try to make of it, we cannot ignore the Great Pyramid's presence; it haunts us and mocks us. William Fix, author of *Pyramid Odyssey,* thinks he knows why: "It is enormous; it is ancient; it is legendary; it is sophisticated; it is the result of great enterprise; it is here for all to see at the crossroads of the earth—and it does not seem to belong to our world."

Seen from the Sphinx at the summer solstice, the sun forms the hieroglyph for "horizon" — a sun setting between two mountains — between the pyramids of Cheops and Chephren.

The Stone Sentinels

Every year on June 21, the date of the summer solstice, people come from all over the world to watch the dazzling spectacle of sunrise over Stonehenge, a circular complex of standing stones, or megaliths, on the Salisbury Plain in southwest England. As the red disk climbs from the horizon, there comes a moment when, to an observer at the center of the circle, the sun seems to be suspended directly above the Heel Stone, a tall marker positioned outside the circle. Not only is the sight a delight to the eye, it is an unfathomable mystery. The stones were emplaced thousands of years ago by prehistoric builders and several serve to indicate where on the horizon the sun and the moon will rise and set at special times throughout the year. But why?

The mystery is intensified by the fact that Stonehenge is just one of several hundred megalithic monuments — some of which are shown on pages 69-79 — sited in Great Britain and Europe. Some stand upright singly; others occur in groups of uprights and horizontals that form portals. Still others, like Stonehenge, stand in circles.

Archeologists agree that these structures were raised between 3500 and 1000 B.C. Astronomers agree that many serve as accurate celestial observatories. Psychics have testified to unearthly experiences in the presence of the stones; and so have many skeptics. Age-old local folklore has endowed the stones with mystic powers to move of their own accord, to whisper, to impregnate the barren, to heal the sick, and to hex the wicked. The reasons why are known only to the spirits, good and evil, believed to reside within and around them.

*The sun hangs over one of thirty-eight megaliths that
stand in a circle at Castlerigg in England. Legend says the stones are men petrified
by the gods; they also serve as astronomical markers.*

The Ring of Brodgar — at 342 feet in diameter, one of the largest stone circles in Great Britain –

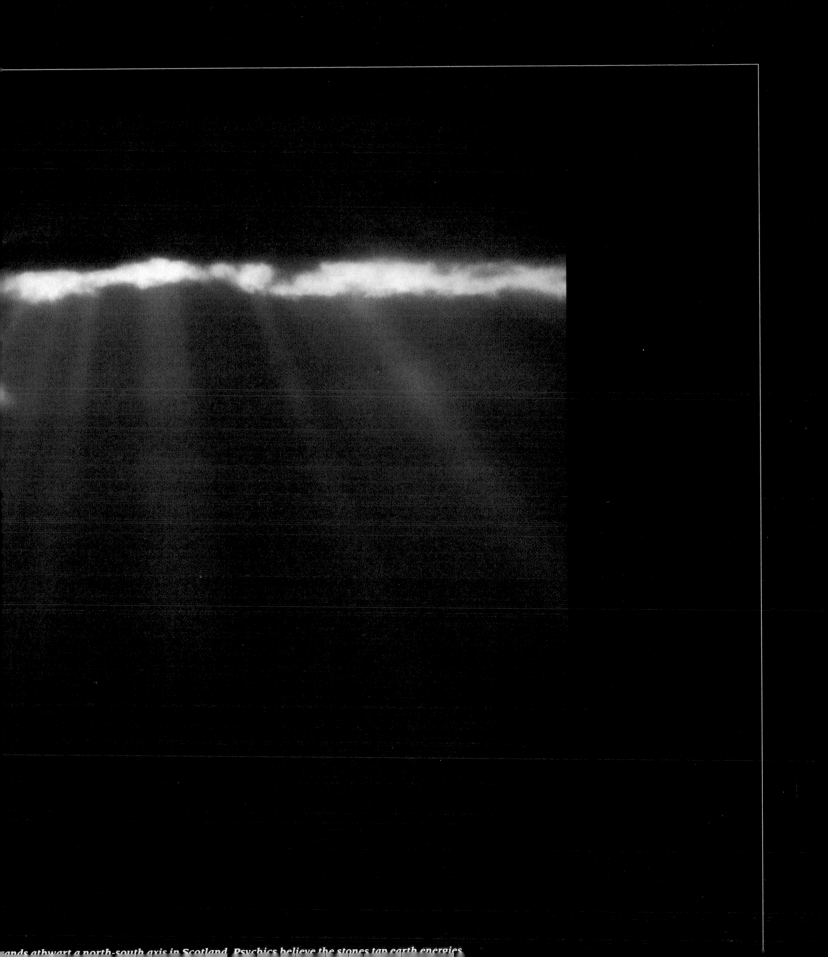

ands athwart a north-south axis in Scotland. Psychics believe the stones tap earth energies.

*The Druids' Altar points heavenward from a stark
limestone upland in southwest Ireland. Megaliths such as this are portal
dolmens; many mark entrances to burial vaults.*

*These stones — from a group of more than 1,000 in
Brittany — proceed inexplicably in eleven lines for half a mile. For centuries,
peasants brought sickly cattle here to be healed.*

Swinside Circle stands on a barren plain in northern England. The stones have sunk somewha

...ver the centuries; legend says that it is the work of the devil, who used to visit nightly,

At Callanish Circle in the Outer Hebrides, a beneficent spirit is believed to make an appeara

the summer solstice. Couples used to come to these stones to make their marriage vows.

Stonehenge looms broodingly over the Salisbury Plain in southwestern England. Dozens

les surround the stones; one says that a race of Irish giants carried the stones from Africa.

CHAPTER 3

The Meaning of the Megaliths

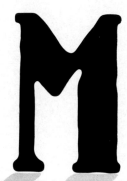

Mounting the roof of an automobile in the Stonehenge parking lot, the young investigator gazed toward the circular cluster of massive upright stones that loomed about 200 yards away. He had come to the famous spot to check for emanations of so-called earth energy, a mystical force venerated by many people who look beyond traditional science for solutions to the mysteries that surround the great stone monument.

The visitor had brought with him a wire antenna bent into an ankh, an ancient Egyptian cross with a loop at the top. Grasping the two-foot-long wire ankh by the loop, he pointed the other end at the giant stones. The result, he reported later, was both startling and painful: A burning jolt of power surged up his arm, hurling him to the ground and knocking him unconscious. When he came to, he found that his arm was paralyzed; it took six months for him to regain its full use. But the experience had proved something to his satisfaction: The earth energy he had come to discover at Stonehenge was real, and it was not to be trifled with.

Poised in isolated splendor on the flat, chalky grassland of England's wind-swept Salisbury Plain some eighty miles west of London, Stonehenge has intrigued investigators such as the ankh wielder for many centuries. Despite all the research and speculation, however, it is still a conundrum. Even the builders of the monument remain unknown: Efforts to prove that they were variously Egyptians, Phoenicians, Greeks, Romans, Druids, Danes, Buddhists, Hindus, Mayans, survivors of the lost island continent of Atlantis, or even visitors from another planet, have all failed.

It is estimated that as many as half of the site's original stones have vanished, with nothing but indentations in the ground to show where they once stood. Many others lie toppled and broken. But as one writer observed 200 years ago, "There is as much of it undemolished as enables us sufficiently to recover its form when it was in its most perfect state. There is enough of every part to preserve the idea of the whole."

The whole is a monument consisting of two concentric rings of upright stones enclosing a pair of nested horseshoe-shaped stone forms. Completing the complex are several solitary stones, including the fancifully named Altar

Stone, Slaughter Stone, and Heel Stone; numerous pits; a shallow circular boundary ditch; and a broad roadway that breaches the ditch at its northeastern rim and connects Stonehenge with the Avon River, about a mile and a half distant.

The feature that gives Stonehenge its distinctive silhouette is a group of tall stone so-called doorways, which describe the outer circle and the outer horseshoe. The circle, about 100 feet in diameter and sixteen feet tall, once consisted of thirty uprights capped by thirty lintels forming an unbroken ring of stone overhead. Even taller than the doorways of the outer circle are the five doorways that once made up the outer horseshoe. Called trilithons (from the Greek words for "three stones"), they range up to nearly thirty feet in height. To erect these massive doorways, the builders somehow had to hoist the huge slabs—weighing perhaps as much as twelve tons each— above the pairs of uprights and then to lower them into place with enough precision that the mortised notches on the undersides of the capstones locked over the stone tenons atop the uprights. It is from these massive lintels that Stonehenge gets its name, variously rendered Stanhengues, Stanenges, Stanheng, Stanhenge, and Stanhenges, from the Old English words for "hanging stone."

Just as the builders of the

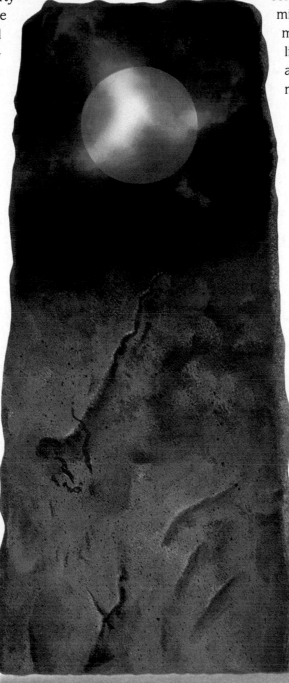

hanging stones have not been identified, so the exact purposes of the place have never been firmly established—although it is believed that the complex almost certainly once served as a temple, one of many such ancient monuments of great stones, or megaliths. By far the greatest concentration of megaliths—some 50,000 in all—is found in western Europe and North Africa, primarily in Britain, Ireland, Spain, Portugal, France, Scandinavia, and Algeria.

These monuments display a wide variety of forms. The simplest are made of single, solitary upright stones known as *menhirs,* Celtic for "long stones." More complicated are groups of menhirs, sometimes arranged in circles or semicircles, and sometimes in vast enfilades stretching for miles. A third type of megalithic monument is the dolmen, a roofed, chamberlike structure that may be freestanding and above ground or enclosed within a massive mound of earth.

Stonehenge finds its place in the second category of megalithic monuments. But it is by no means the largest or the most ambitiously engineered of Britain's stoneworks and earthworks. Prehistoric Silbury Hill in nearby Avebury, to mention just one imposing example, is an artificial mound 130 feet high that is spread out over five and a half acres. Yet among all of them, none is better known, more extensively studied, or more subjected to flights of imagination and scientific speculation than Stonehenge. It stands, as novelist Henry James wrote, "as lonely in history as it does on the great plain."

Stonehenge is built primarily of bluestone, a type of blue-tinted dolerite, and sarsen, a variety of sandstone harder than granite. The bluestones, of which there were eighty or more slabs originally, have been traced to a Welsh quarry about 130 miles northwest of Salisbury Plain; the sarsen slabs were brought from the Marlborough Downs, about twenty miles north of the site. Since wheeled vehicles were unknown in Britain during the time of Stonehenge's construction, the long-distance transportation involved in moving these massive rocks—some of them weighing as much as fifty tons—is among the more astonishing feats accomplished by Stonehenge's builders and one that has given rise to many conjectures.

An exact chronology of the construction is unknown, owing to the scarcity of data from the site and the margin of error inherent in archeological dating techniques. The best scientific guess is that Stonehenge was built in at least four stages, stretching across the centuries between 3100 and 1100 B.C. Not one but a series of ancient peoples contributed to the monument's construction, as evidenced in the varying choices of building materials and methods and also in the differing ultimate visions of Stonehenge. Archeologists believe that in the first phase of construction the monument consisted of a simple circular embankment enclosing a few wooden poles and upright slabs, including the Heel Stone. The second phase was marked by the erection of two rows of bluestones forming a crescent at the center of the site. The doorways and trilithons were created in phase three, and in phase four, about 1100 B.C., the bluestones were reset and the roadway was extended.

Sometime thereafter, Stonehenge seems to have gone into decline, its sacred ground untended and largely unnoticed. Then about A.D. 1130, it was rescued from oblivion by the English clergyman Henry of Huntingdon, who set about to tell his countrymen just what an enigmatic place it was. In his *History of the English,* Henry wrote of "Stanenges, where

stones of wonderful size have been erected after the manner of doorways . . . and no one can conceive how such great stones have been so raised aloft, or why they were built there."

Henry's remarks unleashed endless waves of speculation, beginning with those of his contemporary Geoffrey of Monmouth. In his *History of the Kings of Britain,* written about 1136, Geoffrey gave his version of how Stonehenge came to be. According to this account, the *Chorea Gigantum,* or Dance of the Giants, as Geoffrey called the massive stone structure, was erected on Salisbury Plain in the fifth century A.D., in the days of Aurelius Ambrosius and his brother Uther Pendragon, father of the legendary King Arthur.

Geoffrey began his chronicle with a war between the Britons, led by Ambrosius, and the Saxons under Hengist, a deeply hated foe who had massacred some 460 unarmed British nobles gathered for a peace parley. After defeating Hengist's army in battle and beheading the Saxon leader for his crime, wrote Geoffrey, Ambrosius went to the monastery near Salisbury where the treacherous Hengist's victims lay buried. Moved to tears at the fate of his faithful earls and princes, Ambrosius determined to raise a monument worthy of the memory of such warriors.

Unable to find carpenters or stonemasons capable of building as fine a memorial as he desired, Ambrosius sent for Merlin, a sage renowned for his prophetic powers and mystical knowledge. Merlin advised him that if he wanted to mark the graves of his paladins with an eternal monument, he should emplace the Dance of the Giants, a grouping of great stones that graced a mountain in Ireland. "For in these stones," Merlin explained, "is a mystery, and a healing virtue against many ailments." According to Merlin, a vanished race of Irish giants had carried the magical stones from distant Africa. Water poured over the stones acquired healing properties, and the giants treated their battle wounds with confections of herbs mixed with the magical waters.

Ambrosius, eager to do as Merlin had suggested, put Uther at the head of an army of 15,000 Britons and dispatched him to Ireland to fetch the miracle-working stones. When Uther and his men reached their destination, they attacked the

A Multipurpose Complex

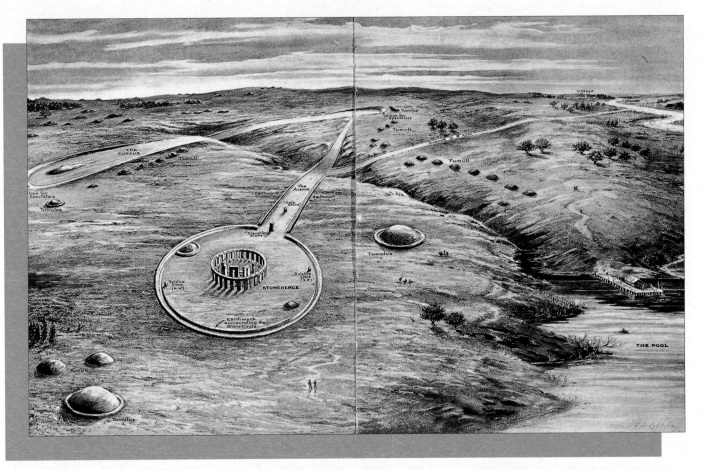

Of all the discarded theories advanced to explain the origins of Stonehenge, one of the most fanciful appeared in an article by one J. G. Gurdon in the *London Illustrated News* of May 13, 1922. Gurdon likened the site to a combination Royal Exchange and Epsom Downs: He thought it had served a dual purpose as trading mart and racetrack — all on sacred ground.

He held that the first arrivals at Stonehenge, those who erected the inner ring, built the place as a temple. The subsequent builders of the outer ring were businessmen who viewed the temple as a natural site for commerce. "Prehistoric folk extended to their temple," he wrote, "that respect which is now commonly paid to the law courts. They were as anxious to avoid conflict with their priests as the modern merchant is to steer clear of lawyers." Thus they felt obliged to bargain without coming to blows.

At first glance, Gurdon's explanation for Stonehenge seemed as sensible as any other. It grew, however, mainly from Gurdon's imagination — and overlooked some important facts. Although articles of gold and bronze found in nearby barrows indicate that trading did take place, the objects date from about 200 years after the completion of Stonehenge. Therefore the site must have had some other purpose that antedated trade.

The rest of his theory, that Stonehenge had been a sports center, relied on even more fanciful reasoning. A nearby earthwork consists of a broad, straight track having a loop at one end and called the *cursus* — Latin for "course." Gurdon decided that it could be nothing other than a racecourse for chariots; the loop enabled cumbersome chariots to turn around and head back down the course. "Sport, like trade," he wrote, "was intimately associated with religion and religious festivals among all primitive people." True enough, but chariots did not appear in Britain until 400 B.C. — and so Gurdon's theory goes the way of many another into archeological limbo.

stones with all manner of devices—but to no avail. Finally Merlin, who had accompanied the expedition, used his magical powers to move the huge stones. In the words of Geoffrey of Monmouth, Merlin "put together his own engines" with which he easily moved the stones to the ships that subsequently transported them to England.

After much celebration and ceremony on Salisbury Plain, Geoffrey wrote, Ambrosius asked Merlin to set up the stones that had been carried away from Ireland. Merlin did so, using the same magical means to place the stones around the burial ground in a circular configuration, just as the vanished giants had arranged them long ago in Ireland. In time, Geoffrey's narrative continued, the magical stone circle erected by Merlin's art became the burial site for both Aurelius and Uther.

Later chroniclers retold Geoffrey's story with variations, and Merlin became firmly entrenched in Stonehenge folklore. By some accounts, the wizard's magic caused the stones to fly through the air all the way from Ireland to Britain. In Elizabethan times, nearly 500 years after the publication of

This drawing by Inigo Jones, a seventeenth-century architect, shows a classically symmetrical Stonehenge. He believed, wrongly, that Stonehenge had been constructed by the Romans.

Geoffrey's *History of the Kings of Britain,* Merlin and the Dance of the Giants became a popular subject for many of London's lesser playwrights. In one melodrama of the period, Merlin vanquishes his father, the devil, and erects Stonehenge in honor of his mortal mother.

Not until the reign of King James I in the early seventeenth century did medieval legend give way to serious investigation of Stonehenge. James paid a visit to the great stones in the summer of 1620 and was so intrigued that he ordered a formal architectural study to satisfy his royal curiosity about the origin and purpose of the mysterious structure. To undertake this Stonehenge study, the monarch chose Inigo Jones, the foremost architect of his day.

Jones had studied painting and architecture in Italy and was well versed in classical principles of design. Obedient to the royal commission, he visited the ancient monument, surveyed the site, and measured the individual stones. Returning to

London, he searched his library of architectural writings to identify Stonehenge's builders. Jones dismissed out of hand Geoffrey of Monmouth's story: "As for that ridiculous Fable," he wrote, "of *Merlin's* transporting the stones out of *Ireland* by Magick, it's an idle conceit." He reviewed and rejected several other ideas about the origin of Stonehenge, including the possibility that ancient Britons may have had a hand in it.

Britain before the Roman invasion, Jones averred, was populated by "savage and barbarous people, knowing no use at all of garments . . . destitute of the knowledge . . . to erect stately structures." Like philosopher Thomas Hobbes, he presumed that life for prehistoric humans in the Isles had been "solitary, poor, nasty, brutish and short"—or, in the words of another seventeenth-century writer, "almost as salvage [savage] as the beasts whose skins were their only rayment . . . 2 or 3 degrees I suppose lesse salvage than the Americans."

Such barbarians, Jones was sure, could not have possessed the esthetic and mathematical sophistication to build anything with as "much Art, order, and proportion" as existed in Stonehenge. His own conclusion: The rocks on Salisbury Plain were the ruins of a temple to the Roman sky-god Coelus, built sometime during the periodic Roman invasion of Britain that began about the start of the Christian era and ended in A.D. 410. "Amongst all the nations of the universe," he declared, only the Romans could have created such a marvel.

After Jones's death in 1652, his disciple and son-in-law John Webb edited the architect's notes on his Roman-origin theory into a volume entitled *The Most Notable Antiquity of Great Britain, Vulgarly Called Stone-Heng, on Salisbury Plain. Restored.* This book, the first devoted exclusively to Stonehenge, was a critical and popular failure. Most copies remained unsold and were destroyed in London's Great Fire of 1666, but it did provoke dissenters to come up with arguments of their own.

One avid reader of Jones's book was Walter Charleton, a learned scholar-physician in the court of King Charles II. In the course of extended correspondence with a Danish antiquarian, Charleton had become convinced that Stonehenge replicated the design of megalithic burial chambers found in Denmark. In a 1663 treatise entitled *Chorea Gigantum, or the Most Famous Antiquity of Great-*

Britain, Vulgarly Called STONE-HENG, Standing on Salisbury Plain, Restored to the DANES, Charleton sought to wrest credit for the stone monument from the Romans and deliver it to the Danish conquerors who had invaded England in Viking times.

Stonehenge, the doctor wrote, had been "erected by the Danes, when they had this Nation in subjection; and principally, if not wholly Design'd to be a Court Royal, or place for the Election and Inauguration of their Kings." Charleton pointed to the crownlike circular layout of Stonehenge as evidence that it had been connected with coronation rituals and suggested that the high stone lintels had provided lofty gathering places for Danish electors. He even ventured the idea that Alfred the Great had been able to defeat the Danes in A.D. 878 because the invaders had come to the battle weakened by overindulgence at celebrations that were held to mark the completion of Stonehenge.

Inaugurating what would become a long tradition of sometimes bitter adversarial relationships among Stonehenge theorists, Charleton accused the late Inigo Jones of being seduced by his imagination to follow "a course highly disingenuous . . . scandalous . . . [deserving] Shame and Discredit." Webb countered soon after with yet another publication, in which he attacked Charleton as "shallow . . . frivo-

lous . . . vain" and Charleton's Danes as practitioners of "Necromancy, Sorcery, Perjury, Treachery, Cruelty and Tyranny: their professions Adultery, rape, rapine, robbery, piracy and sacrilege; their recreations homicide, filicide, fratricide, patricide, matricide and regicide."

These spirited exchanges kept the antiquarian community engaged for a time. But another more controversial—and ultimately more durable—view was soon to emerge, shouldering aside all previous contenders. Stonehenge, so the new theorists proposed, was a temple built by the Druids.

Druids were native Englishmen, or nearly so. They made up the elite priestly class of Celts that had swept westward from the continent to populate Britain as long ago as 2000 B.C. The little that is known about them—or about the Celts in general—comes chiefly from the writings of their Greek and Roman contemporaries; the priests themselves seem to have had little use for written language, perhaps fearing it might allow their special learning to fall into the wrong hands.

What made the Druid connection to Stonehenge so controversial was the reputed bloodiness of their religious ceremonies. How could men with such repugnant practices have produced such a sublime work? Many of the classical chron-

The Druid sacrifice of the vernal Equinox.

Stukeley delin. 1759.

ing "consisting more in contemplation than practice," not the sort of studies he considered "proper to inform the judgement of an Architect. . . . In a word, therefore let it suffice, Stoneheng was no work of the Druids."

Forceful as they were, such arguments did not dissuade John Aubrey. A fellow of the Royal Society, Aubrey was an author whose writings ranged across such diverse fields as biography, folklore, and antiquarian studies. He was born in 1626 in the village of Easton Pierse, about thirty miles from Stonehenge, and took a keen interest in the multitude of ancient stone monuments bristling across the countryside of Britain. His studies of Stonehenge identified an outer ring just inside the earthen trench; the ring consisted of small, barely visible, man-made cavities that had previously gone unnoticed. Known ever since as the Aubrey Holes, these diggings measure up to six feet in diameter and two to four feet in depth, with flat bottoms. They were filled in with rubble, including charred bones that Aubrey took to be human.

His interest piqued, Aubrey examined Jones's analysis in *Stone-Heng Restored* and concluded that the architect-author had withheld data to frame "the monument to his own hypoth-

iclers present the Druids as a sinister fraternity, dedicated—as the Roman historian Publius Cornelius Tacitus wrote—to "inhuman superstitions and barbarous rites." Julius Caesar, who wrote extensively on the Druids in his *Gallic Wars,* claimed that they made human sacrifices to their gods by constructing immense wicker cages in human form, "whose limbs, woven out of twigs, they fill with living men and set on fire, and the men perish in a sheet of flame."

Diodorus Siculus, Caesar's contemporary, reflected a similar view. He wrote of Druid rituals in which the priests "kill a man by a knife-stab in the region above his midriff, and after his fall they foretell the future by the convulsions of his limbs and the pouring of his blood." And Tacitus reported further that when Britons were victorious in battle, "This inhuman people were accustomed to shed the Blood of their Prisoners on their Altars, and consult the Gods over the reeking Bowels of Men."

Inigo Jones, in his cataloguing of peoples who could not have built Stonehenge, also took a swipe at the Celtic priests: "Concerning the Druids," he wrote, "certainly Stoneheng could not be builded by them, in regard, I find no mention, they were at any time either studious in architecture . . . or skilful in anything else conducing thereunto." Jones allowed that the Druids may have been philosophers and astronomers, as Julius Caesar had mentioned, but those were branches of learn-

The Druid sacrifice of Yule-tide.

Stukeley delin. 1759.

The Druid sacrifice of the autumnal equinox.

W. Stukeley f. 1759. fine vitris.

Once he laid eyes on Stonehenge, Stukeley could not stay away. "It pleases like a magical spell," he wrote. The spell continued to work on him as he returned to the site repeatedly during the early 1720s. On one occasion he and a friend brought a ladder with them, climbed one of the doorways and strolled about on top of the lintel, surveying the rest of Stonehenge from above. They later picnicked on their high perch, enjoyed a smoke, and left their pipes behind as mementos of their jaunt when they climbed down to return home.

Not all of Stukeley's visits to the ancient stones were purely pleasure trips, however. He was also gathering data for a Stonehenge book he planned to write. He took exact measurements of the stones and their ground plan, explored earthworks in the vicinity, and did some excavating —being careful not to dig too near the stones lest he accidentally cause them to topple.

Even before Stukeley began his Stonehenge research, he and a group of friends had founded a social club they called the Society of Roman Knights. The members grandly devoted themselves to protecting Britain's Roman archeological heritage against "time, Goths, and barbarians," and each of the knights took a fanciful name from the Roman or Celtic past. After casting about for a suitable namesake, Stukeley finally picked a fabled French Druid high priest called Chyndonax. Choosing that name was his first step toward embracing the

esis, which is much differing from the thing itself." Aubrey thought no better of his friend Charleton's Danish theory, nor of any other attribution that turned foreign invaders into Stonehenge builders. Britain's stone antiquities, Aubrey wrote in a counterargument entitled *Monumenta Britannica,* were so widely distributed in areas hardly touched by successive waves of invaders that they could only have been constructed by native Britons. Admitting that he was "gropeing into the dark" to reach his conclusion, Aubrey said of Stonehenge and other megalithic structures that there was "clear evidence these monuments were Pagan Temples" and a "probability that these were temples of the Druids."

Aubrey's cautious thesis remained unpublished at his death in 1697. But twenty years later, the manuscript of *Monumenta Britannica* came to the attention of William Stukeley, a physician, an antiquarian, and an orthodox Christian.

Stukeley had first become excited about megaliths when he toured several stone antiquities—but not Stonehenge—in 1710. One site, he remarked cautiously, might have been "an heathen temple of our Ancestors, perhaps in the Druids' time." By the time he got to see Britain's most famous megalith, nine years later, he had become thoroughly enchanted with Druidism and with the lore of Stonehenge. He had even undertaken to build a pair of precise replicas, showing the structure in both "its present ruins" and its "pristine state."

The Midsummer sacrifice of the Druids.

Stukeley delin. 1759.

Druid identity in which he would ultimately submerge himself. By the time he finally published his Stonehenge book in 1740, Stukeley had given up his medical career to become a minister of the Church of England, and his secular interest in British megaliths had been replaced by a sense of religious mission. His book, entitled *Stonehenge, a Temple Restored to the British Druids,* attempted to fit the author's version of Druidism into "a chronological history of the origin and progress of true religion, and of idolatry." According to Stukeley's theory, there was an unbroken religious tradition linking the Old Testament patriarchs, the Druids, and the Church of England. The Druids, Stukeley proclaimed in his book, were spiritual ancestors of whom modern Anglicans could be proud. They were wise mystics and natural philosophers who had "advanced their inquires . . . to such heights as should make our moderns ashamed, to wink in the sunshine of learning and religion."

It is true that these ancient sages had practiced human sacrifice, but Stukeley was able to explain away the embarrassing excess as "a most extraordinary act of superstition," perhaps attributable to a misunderstanding of the Old Testament story in which the Lord commands Abraham to sacrifice Isaac. Stonehenge, in Stukeley's reconstruction of Britain's religious past, was nothing less than "the metropolitan Church of the Chief Druid of Britain . . . the *locus consecratus* where they met at some great festivals of the year, as well as to perform the extraordinary sacrifices and religious rites."

After finishing *Stonehenge Restored to the Druids,* Stukeley continued to develop his theories of ancient religion, studying other megaliths and planning a multivolume treatise on what he called the patriarchal Christianity practiced by the

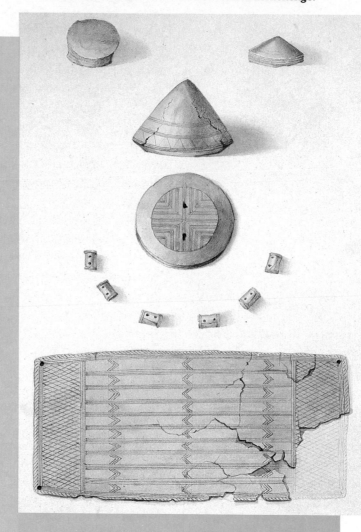

Gold studs, beads, and other jewelry found in a barrow by Sir Richard Colt Hoare look Mycenaean, which led Sir Richard to believe that Greeks had erected Stonehenge.

Druids as he imagined them. He produced only one further volume on the subject, a study of the megaliths at nearby Avebury, in which he argued that its great ring of stones was just one part of a massive earth-and-stone sculpture laid out by the Druids across miles of countryside. By connecting megaliths on a map the way one might connect stars to form constellations, Stukeley discovered the sinuous shape of a serpent passing through a circle. He imputed profound religious symbolism to this image, calling the megalithic serpent sculpture a "noble monument to our ancestors' piety."

Apart from his Druid speculations, one of Stukeley's most enduring contributions to the study of Stonehenge was his observation that the axis of the complex structure, as defined by the physical orientation of several key features, pointed directly "northeast, where abouts the sun rises, when the days are longest." Subsequent observers have noted that the megalith called the Heel Stone, which stands just outside the circles' entrance, aligns with the center of Stonehenge to mark almost the exact spot on the horizon where the sun rises on the day of the summer solstice. But Stukeley was the first to suggest that prehistoric Britons built their megaliths with precise astronomical alignments in mind.

Like Geoffrey of Monmouth's Merlin story, Stukeley's neo-Druidism was absorbed into the body of Stonehenge mythology and repeated with embellishments by many other enthusiasts of megalith lore. Architect John Wood, renowned as a principal designer of the eighteenth-century reconstruction of the city of Bath, studied Stonehenge at length, declaring it "the great sanctuary of the ARCHPROPHET of *Britain.*" Wood concluded that the numbers and arrangements of the stones corresponded to lunar cycles and that the stone encirclement was none other than the temple to the moon-goddess Diana. Wood was succeeded by a Druidophile named Henry Hurle, who took the revivalist movement to its logical extreme, founding in 1781 what he called the Ancient Order of Druids. This was to be only the first of many neo-Druid sects that would choose Stonehenge as the site of initiation ceremonies and other religious observances.

The close of the eighteenth century saw no end to the fascination with Stonehenge and other ancient structures in the area. A number of nineteenth-century investigators had interests somewhat different from those of their predecessors, however. The prosperous baronet Sir Richard Colt Hoare, for example, devoted himself to overseeing and financing the excavation of hundreds of ancient barrows, or earth mounds, many of them in the immediate vicinity of Stonehenge. Some of the artifacts that were unearthed in these old burial sites convinced Colt Hoare and his associates that the barrows as well as Stonehenge had been raised before the Roman invasion of Britain.

Even Charles Darwin, the great theorist of biological evolution, traveled to Stonehenge in his old age. His aim was to learn something of the activity of earthworms by gauging how far the monument's fallen stones had settled into the soil. In 1881, the year of his death, Darwin published his findings in a curious book entitled *The Formation of Vegetable Mould, through the Action of Worms.*

While megalith scholars bristled at the destructive diggings of Colt Hoare and other diligent excavators, they saved the bulk of their ire for the romantic enthusiasms of neo-Druidism. Such links with magic and the occult inevitably led to a scholarly backlash, particularly among the newly emerging breed of professional archeologists who sought to dissociate themselves from the amateur gentlemen antiquarians of the past. By the end of the nineteenth century, support for the Druids among the scientific establishment had been replaced with contempt; suggestions that the Celtic priests might be connected with Stonehenge were dismissed out of hand. Then

the respected British astronomer Sir J. Norman Lockyer got into the act and demonstrated that there was, in fact, much common ground between the scientists and the romantics.

Lockyer was as much an insider in the world of science as the Druid revivalists of the 1700s had been outsiders. Along with his many other accomplishments—which included the founding of the prestigious scientific journal *Nature*—he had determined in the 1890s that the orientations of the Great Pyramid of Giza and other ancient Egyptian structures correspond with the periodic positions of the sun and several important stars.

In 1901, seven years after publishing these findings, Lockyer turned his attention to the ancient megaliths of his own country. Working with a friend, astronomer and archeologist F. C. Penrose, Lockyer went first to Stonehenge, then on to other megalithic sites to make the same kinds of astronomical observations and calculations he had made in Egypt. In 1906, he published his conclusions in a book entitled *Stonehenge and Other British Stone Monuments Astronomically Considered.*

The volume could have been called, with a nod to Jones, Charleton, and Stukeley, *Stonehenge Restored to the Astronomers.* In it, Lockyer made the controversial claim that prehistoric Britons, ''astronomer-priests'' of the second and third millennia B.C., had been the architects of Britain's mysterious stone monuments. He further asserted that these ancients were easily the astronomical equals of their Egyptian contemporaries and that they had planned Stonehenge as a kind of astronomical calendar, with its stones arranged to mark crucial points in the cyclical movements of the sun, moon, and stars. The implications were clear: Not only had ancient Britons mastered some astonishingly complex feats of long-term observation, calculation, and scientific record keeping, but the Druids, inheritors of their science and philosophy, were legitimate occupants of Stonehenge after all.

Lockyer was too much a giant in the field of astronomy to be ignored altogether. But the majority of archeologists attacked his conclusions and Druidism as well. His pioneering theories found no adherents, and decades would pass be-

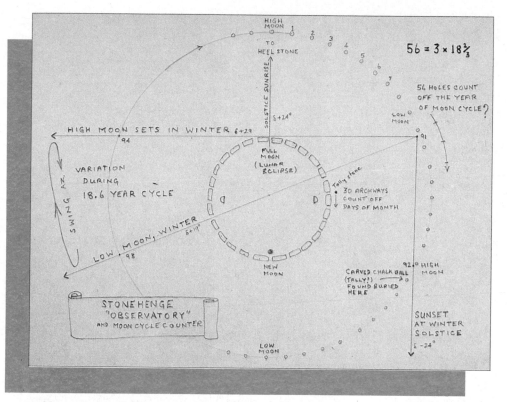

In this pencil sketch, astronomer Gerald Hawkins shows how ancient Britons could have predicted lunar eclipses by taking sightings from just inside the circumference of Stonehenge's Aubrey Holes — the fifty-six stoneless pits in the outer circle.

fore the astronomer's work gained recognition and respect.

This process began with the research of astronomer Gerald S. Hawkins, a British-born professor at Boston University. Using a computer to check the movements of heavenly bodies against the positions of stones, Aubrey Holes, and other Stonehenge features, Hawkins discovered what he believed to be a total correlation with the extreme seasonal positions of the rising and setting of the sun and the moon. His computer analysis convinced him that the odds against so many astronomically significant placements occurring purely by chance were greater than a million to one.

Hawkins published his seemingly definitive findings about Stonehenge's astronomical alignments in 1963—appropriately enough in *Nature* magazine. Eight months later,

writing in the same journal, he took his argument even further and suggested that Stonehenge was a kind of Stone Age computer, designed to predict lunar eclipses. The timing of eclipses, Hawkins said, is related to an 18.6-year cycle of lunar movements across the night sky, and he maintained that Stonehenge's ancient astronomers would have been able to track this pattern for three cycles by moving stone markers around the circle of fifty-six Aubrey Holes. In 1965, Hawkins published an expanded version of his theory of Stonehenge in a book boldly entitled *Stonehenge Decoded.*

The book generated considerable public discussion, and its conclusions were hotly debated among Hawkins's fellow scientists—sometimes in tones reminiscent of the bombast generated centuries before by Inigo Jones's pioneering theories about Stonehenge. The prehistorian R.J.C. Atkinson, whose 1956 book *Stonehenge* had disputed Lockyer's archeoastronomical findings, attacked Hawkins's *Stonehenge Decoded* as a "tendentious, arrogant, slipshod, and unconvincing" piece of work.

But Fred Hoyle, a Cambridge University astronomy professor, was more hospitable to Hawkins's theory about the megalithic site. Certain features of Stonehenge, Hoyle agreed, seemed to point to a previously unsuspected level of astronomical sophistication on the part of the structure's builders. "A veritable Newton or Einstein must have been at work," he marveled. "It demands a level of intellectual attainment [that is] orders of magnitude higher than the standard to be expected from a community of primitive farmers."

If Hawkins had startled orthodox scholars with his vision of Stonehenge, there was an even greater shock to come. For at the same time that debate was raging over his findings in *Stonehenge Decoded,* a particularly dogged mega-

*This megalith in Cornwall was considered a healing stone;
sick children were passed through the hole to be cured. The upright stone in the
distance is thought to have served for astronomical observations.*

lith investigator continued to gather data that would eventually win over some of archeoastronomy's most stubborn foes.

Scottish engineer Alexander Thom, a professor at Oxford University until his retirement in 1961, had been surveying ancient stone structures since before World War II. Not until 1973, however, did he make his first visit to Stonehenge. By that time, he had published two books—*Megalithic Sites in Britain* and *Megalithic Lunar Observatories*—in which he claimed to have identified an intricate network of prehistoric astronomical sites. He had found more, Thom said, than mere alignments between individual megaliths and the cycles of the sun, moon, and stars. He had also discovered many pairs of structures, sometimes miles apart, that could be lined up like the front and rear sights of a rifle to make important astronomical observations.

When he finally brought his surveying equipment to Stonehenge, Thom concluded that this most famous of all megaliths had been erected as a central rear sight from which prehistoric astronomers could take bearings on six different front sights. The nearest of these Thom identified as a burial mound just a mile southeast of Stonehenge; the farthest was an earthwork on a knoll nine miles to the northwest.

Thom's theory held that megalith builders throughout western Europe constructed their separate monuments according to certain common standards. Chief among these standards was a unit of measurement Thom called the "megalithic yard," a 2.72-foot length he calculated by measuring and comparing the diameters of numerous stone circles. He also found these early builders to be knowledgeable about geometry as well as astronomy: They had laid out their structures in six regularly proportioned shapes, displaying an understanding of Pythagorean geometric principles centuries before the birth of the great Greek mathematician Pythagoras.

Scholars such as Atkinson, who had lashed out at Lockyer and Hawkins, might have been expected to savage Thom as well. But when the *Journal for the History of Astronomy* published Thom's Stonehenge findings in 1975, Atkinson studied the engineer's carefully compiled data and confessed that he had to recant his previous statements. "It is important that nonarchaeologists should understand how disturbing to archaeologists are the implications of Thom's work," Atkinson wrote, "because [his opinions] do not fit the conceptual model of the prehistory of Europe which has been current during the whole of the present century." But in the face of Thom's overwhelming evidence, Atkinson was prepared to abandon that prevailing vision of prehistory; there was simply no denying the case Thom had made for the astronomical abilities of the supposedly backward primeval Britons.

Archeoastronomy had, at last, arrived. And its acceptance by the scientific establishment lent aid and comfort to many nonscientists who had developed their own ideas about Stonehenge and other megaliths. If one previously scorned theory could be vindicated with a virtual stroke of the pen, who could say that others could not be similarly redeemed?

Probably the best known of these alternative archeology theories originated in the 1920s with a Herefordshire businessman named Alfred Watkins. Watkins claimed to have discovered a grid of straight lines—he called them leys, from the Saxon word for "meadow" or "cleared strip of land"—that crisscrossed the Welsh border countryside he knew so well.

These leys, Watkins asserted, were man-made trackways that linked megaliths, burial mounds, and other significant sites, some of which are positioned on hilltops as so-called initial points. Altogether the leys and points formed, in his poetic phrase, "a fairy chain, stretched from mountain peak to mountain peak as far as the eye could reach." He deduced that leys marked ancient traders' tracks initially laid down between 4000 and 2000 B.C. but subsequently abandoned and forgotten. And he found that many early Christian churches had been built on leys, presumably because they were constructed to replace previous pagan sites of sanctity.

Watkins set forth his ideas in three books, including *Early British Trackways* (1922) and *The Old Straight Track* (1925). Mainstream science had no interest in his ley theories, but Watkins found his share of followers. In the late 1920s, these hardy believers banded together to form the Old Straight

Tracking the Earth's Energies

"It's easy to find literature today dramatically claiming that megaliths possess energies and weird forces," says Paul Devereux, a longtime student of the prehistoric stone structures. "But such speculation comes cheap and easy. The real front-line research involves more sweat than glory, more grind than results. What findings there are have been hard won."

That kind of no-nonsense determination has characterized Devereux's attempts to unravel the secrets of the hundreds of megaliths dotting the British countryside. He and his co-workers believe that standing stones such as those at Stonehenge may act as conductors of an inexplicable force known as earth energy, channeling it in invisible streams that coincide with leys, or alignments.

To study this so-called earth energy, Devereux in 1978 launched a two-pronged assault involving both physical and psychic research methods. The project's physical program stressed the utilization of the latest scientific technology, such as electronic scanners that are designed to detect minute traces of all kinds of energy; plans for the less orthodox psychic probing included such techniques as the use of dowsers to locate streams of energy. Devereux called his undertaking the Dragon Project, drawing the name from an ancient Chinese symbol for terrestrial currents. As a first

step, Devereux and the project members established a field base at the Rollright Stones, a megalithic site about twenty miles northwest of Oxford, England. Since time out of mind, there had been reports of weird occurrences and supernatural happenings at Rollright. Once, a man had been found tied to one of the stones with his throat cut, and on Devereux's own initial visit to the stones, he surprised a group of occultists in the midst of a ritual. Dragon Project volunteers—many of them recruited by an advertisement in a journal called *The Ley Hunter*—freely gave their time and energy to the research project, undeterred by limited funds and even the theft of some of their equipment. "We were," one of the project members noted ruefully, "a typically British, shoestring affair."

Nonetheless, their efforts produced results almost immediately. Strange energy readings were detected and recorded. Eerily, these readings usually began from eight to twenty minutes before sunrise and ended abruptly from one to two hours after. Some of the energies were identified as ultrasound, a tone beyond the normal range of human hearing, as in a dog whistle.

Geiger counters were used by Devereux and his co-workers to measure radiation. Tests taken inside the circle of stones showed that Rollright had slightly higher counts of radiation than

Dowser Frank Connors uses angle rods to test for energy currents (left). Dowsers claim to have detected corkscrews of energy around some megaliths (above).

nonmegalithic sites in England.

These findings reminded one of the project members that in the United States and Australia, where Indians and aborigines are involved with landrights issues with their governments, uranium deposits had been discovered under their sacred sites. A French writer added that in France the areas with the highest density of megaliths very often correspond with uranium-rich zones.

From these facts, some researchers have been able to infer that prehistoric megalith builders may well have been attracted—perhaps without knowing it—to sites that are naturally radioactive.

But the most interesting of the studies may be the one that involved geomagnetism. A device known as a magnetometer, which monitors the earth's magnetic field, was used by the Dragon Project. Devereux reported a particular stone showed a high magnetic field and rapid fluctuations of the magnetic energy, seeming to confirm the belief of several dowsers that megaliths are often associated with geomagnetic peculiarities.

This discovery suggested to Devereux and his colleagues that at least one folk belief long associated with all megaliths—that they have healing properties—may be rooted in fact. It is known, for example, that throughout the centuries, locals have come to the stones in the hopes of mending broken bones. Oddly enough, modern hospitals commonly use electromagnetism to speed up the healing process of bone fractures.

Another of the Dragon Project findings—one that engaged both the physical and the psychic branches of the research—took place when, according to Devereux, a dowser found himself able to cause marked fluctuations in a sensitive voltmeter simply by placing his hand on particularly energy-sensitive areas of one of the stones. Nondowsers, however, proved unable to repeat the effect.

Perhaps strangest of all, Devereux maintains that several Dragon Proj-

Paul Devereux, director of the Dragon Project, readies his magnetometer at the Maen Llia stone in Wales. Folklore says that the stone regularly travels to a nearby stream for a drink of water.

ect researchers, each acting independently, reported inexplicable sightings in the environs of Rollright Stones: A car, a large furry animal, and an entire gypsy caravan seemed to materialize on a road near the stones and then disappeared without a trace. Devereux speculates that increased radiation detected at the site may have induced mild hallucinations.

In the judgment of Devereux and his co-workers, the various findings of the still-active Dragon Project support the belief that the builders of the megaliths could sense changes in the earth's energy fields that led them to places of power.

"The stones have begun to reveal some of their secrets," he says, "but we are still in a megalithic kindergarten. We have much yet to learn."

Track Club and to publish a magazine called *The Ley Hunter*. For all his apparent originality, Watkins was not alone in his discovery of leylike tracks. Various earlier antiquarians had reported the alignment of ancient sites: In America in the 1850s, William Pidgeon had noted alignments of Indian mounds *(page 122)*. Simultaneous with Watkins's work, German regional planner Dr. Josef Heinsch was studying in his country the alignments of ancient churches with "holy hills," and Wilhelm Teudt was investigating what he called "holy lines" knifing across the German countryside. None of these investigators was aware of the work of his contemporaries.

Later researchers would discover systems of straight lines in the Andes that also are similar to Watkins's leys. The most famous of these are the Nazca lines in Peru, tracks on the desert that pass without deviation over hills and through a valley for up to six miles. Even more closely linked to the ley concept are the lines in western Bolivia known as *taki'is,* a word understood by local Aymaran Indians to mean "straight lines of holy places." These alignments can extend for up to twenty miles, although most are considerably shorter.

In 1976, British writer-explorer Tony Morrison surveyed these Bolivian lines with special infrared measuring equipment and found them to be amazingly straight. But the original purpose of such precision remains a mystery: The only clue came from an Indian woman who told Morrison that the lines were "spirit paths." Adding to the puzzle is the fact that many early Spanish colonial churches stand on these lines, a siting coincidence matching that reported by Watkins in Britain. The following year, Morrison used infrared photography to find straight lines, or *ceques,* radiating out from the Inca Temple of the Sun in Cuzco, Peru.

Although Watkins's Old Straight Trackers Club had faded from view around the time of World War II, interest in the leys revived markedly in the 1960s, spurred by Thom's findings and the resulting upswing in the fortunes of archeoastronomy. One ley enthusiast went beyond Watkins's original theory to declare that leys are "a striking network of lines of subtle force across Britain, and elsewhere on spaceship Earth, understood and marked in prehistoric times by men of wisdom and cosmic consciousness." According to this view, leys carry a mysterious earth energy that was known to the megalith builders, who somehow stored or harnessed it in the great stones they erected. Stonehenge, where two of the most prominent leys intersect, figures in such theories as a focal point of energies, as a sort of storage battery or sending-and-receiving station tied into a mysterious power grid.

For many ley researchers, a fundamental tool is the dowsing rod, a forked rod usually fashioned from the branch of a living tree, which diviners traditionally use to sense underground streams and to site water wells. The rod, held before the dowser as he walks, is believed to dip downward to a water source; the greater the volume, the stronger the pull on the rod. Such an apparatus first was used for investigating leys in the 1930s by French dowsers, who claimed that crossings of underground streams occurred along leys under certain ancient sites, particularly under megaliths. Over recent decades, a number of master dowsers in Britain, America, and parts of Europe have concentrated on dowsing energy manifestations around standing stones and between local groups of megaliths. The most notable such effort, perhaps, is the Dragon Project headed by journalist Paul Devereux *(pages 96-97)*.

Some ley hunters have been struck by the high correlation between megalithic sites and reported UFO sightings, arguing that places such as Stonehenge may have been built as earth markers and landing places for extraterrestrial visitors. John Michell, one of the more extravagant proponents of this theory, has gone so far as to propose that Stonehenge was intended to represent the shape of an ancient extraterrestrial vehicle whose highly advanced occupants seemed godlike to the Stone Age Britons. The monument, he contends, is "a pattern of the sacred disc, built to attract this object for which man felt such a yearning." Developing his theory in a book entitled *The Flying Saucer Vision,* Michell says that when seen from above, Stonehenge's form "exactly reflects the conventional image of the flying saucer. . . . There is the well defined outer rim consisting of a low bank and ditch. Inside this are the

Aubrey holes . . . just like the portholes so often reported in flying saucers. . . . In the center is the perfect stone circle of the raised cabin, enclosing the horseshoe-shaped trilithon construction which appears above the surrounding rim like a dome or cockpit. The smaller bluestones stand inside the circle and are visible through its openings. . . . It seems likely that these stones which were brought from Wales were originally set up elsewhere to mark places of contact between men and gods and that they were taken to Stonehenge to represent the gods themselves inside their vehicle."

UFO sightings have been commonly reported in the vicinity of Stonehenge; several have been claimed at the site itself. In February 1954, a photographer who had been taking pictures of Stonehenge discovered on developing his film that every shot showed "a column of light"—alleged to be some sort of mysterious aircraft—mounting from the stones into the sky. In 1968, a UFO investigator reported seeing at Stonehenge a flying object that at some point "blacked out entirely," then turned into a ring of fire that seemed to shoot from the stones; as observers tried to approach it, the craft soared away into the skies. In October 1977, a squadron of UFOs was reported moving in rapidly changing formation over Stonehenge, with some of the supposed spacecraft dematerializing as observers watched. This strange heavenly activity was said to have interfered with the operation of magnetic compasses and a portable television set, and a searchlight turned on the

Spiral carvings adorn a stone outside a tomb in Newgrange, Ireland. Some archeologists believe Newgrange was a temple to the sun and the spirals represent its rebirth at the winter solstice.

Modern Druids celebrate the summer solstice at Stonehenge. No evidence links the original Druids t

...he site, but their self-styled descendants still gather ritually to mark the changing of the seasons.

UFOs was rendered useless by some inexplicable force that caused it to fade out before it could illuminate the flying objects. Observers did, however, succeed in capturing this multiple UFO sighting with a movie camera, and a film of the event was broadcast later that year on British television.

Perhaps even stranger than reports of UFO activity is the story of a group of visitors who told of hearing a "strange clicking sound from the stones." As they fled in fear, they heard the sound change into "a strange whirring noise" that "shot heavenwards as if a giant catherine wheel [pinwheel] had gone spinning upwards." Shortly thereafter they saw a vision of a yellow-clad woman wearing what looked like an ancient Egyptian headdress. This apparition, together with what they had heard near the stones, left the visitors with the sense that they had witnessed "some sort of struggle between good and evil."

This incident might be seen as a manifestation of yet another phenomenon claimed to occur at megalithic sites: the presence of psychic emissions, or so-called memory fields. A number of people who claim to be gifted with psychic powers that make them able to discern the afterimages of certain events of ancient times and who practice an arcane art called psychometry have investigated the sites to see if they could pick up visions of the original inhabitants. One such psychic, after experiencing the "thoughtforms" of a stone circle in Ireland, reported to have seen priests with yellow robes moving among the stones. "They draw power from these stones," the psychic explained, adding that they used the power to understand the sun and the moon. The psychic also sensed that the priests eventually lost their hold on the place and were succeeded by others who carried out "horrible things."

Another psychometrist has reported seeing cosmic energy earthing or grounding itself in the center of a stone circle in Cumbria, England. The energy appeared vividly as "a veritable pillar of living power . . . fiery mother-of-pearl, opalescent and tinged with an inner colouring of rose." Apparently, Stonehenge itself has not been fertile ground for the psychometrists, though they will no doubt continue to probe for memory fields in the area.

Still another means of discovering the essential truths of Stonehenge has been argued imaginatively and at length by the American Donald Cyr. Cyr maintains that the answers are to be found in the patterns of atmospheric halos, which, he says, allow us to " 'X-ray' the very minds of our prehistoric ancestors and deduce what they were thinking about and why." According to his complex analysis, the skies over ancient Salisbury Plain were somehow capped by a canopy of ice crystals that refract the sun's rays to form atmospheric halos, including many of twenty-two degrees and of forty-six degrees. Such halos, Cyr contends, were "seen on a daily basis when Stonehenge was designed. . . . A semicircle with a precise 22 degree radius (dictated by the behavior of ice-crystal refraction at this angle) would just fit over the four Sarcen stones and their lintels." Cyr links these halos with the position, height, notching, and curvatures of each of the stones in relation to the yearly progression of the sun.

Such things as atmospheric halos may sound outlandish—but so, once, did archeoastronomy. And no one can predict with absolute certainty that leys or other alternative archeology theories about Stonehenge will not someday win the same scientific approval. It is certain, however, that Stonehenge will go on capturing the imagination of the general public.

And it is just as certain that scientists and mystics alike will continue to study the megaliths on Salisbury Plain with keen interest, striving as they have for centuries to unlock the monument's many secrets. New theories will be added to the many extraordinary ones already proposed to explain Stonehenge, and advanced technologies will be brought in to supplement the laser beams, Geiger counters, computers, and infrared cameras already in use.

But it is possible that Stonehenge's mysteries will never entirely yield to human inquiry, that some questions about the monument's origin and purposes are destined to remain unanswered. Perhaps, after all, the definitive word on Stonehenge was given by the seventeenth-century naval official and diarist Samuel Pepys. In 1668, Pepys visited the stones and noted in his diary: "God knows what their use was!"

Along the Leys

A surprisingly high number of supernatural experiences are said to occur on or near leys — those remarkable alignments of prehistoric barrows, dolmens, stone circles, pagan altars, and medieval churches. Some visitors to these sites have visions of historic figures reenacting the deeds they performed in life. Others say they feel the physical presence of a strange force that they cannot see or identify but that lifts them from the ground, strikes them, shoves them about, or suffuses them with inexplicable moods. No one seems to be able to explain the reasons for these things — but statisticians, engineers, dowsers, UFO enthusiasts, psychics, and astroarcheologists have all had a hand in trying.

Some researchers believe that leys are located along channels of geophysical power. They suspect that ancient people sensed a pulsating energy coursing through the earth and built their monuments at sites where the energy was strongest. Some investigators believe that the intersections of leys form so-called nodes, which they say are the points where the energy is particularly strong and able to set off psychic phenomena.

Explanations remain elusive, but many psychic episodes have been reported to have occurred on the leys. Some of them are recounted on the following pages.

A Phantom Army at Loe Bar

Late one afternoon in August 1936, a sixteen-year-old named Stephen Jenkins was exploring on Loe Bar, a stretch of the Cornish coast near where King Arthur is said to have met his death. As Jenkins gazed about, he was astonished to see a host of medieval warriors in chain mail appear before him. Some wore cloaks of red, others white, others black; their horses were caparisoned to match. One soldier in the center stood, hands on his sword, staring at the spot where Jenkins stood. Eager to have a closer look, Jenkins stepped forward, but as he did, the army vanished as suddenly as it had appeared.

That single experience was incredible enough. But when Jenkins returned to the same spot thirty-eight years later, this time with a map in his hands and his wife at his side, the same vision reappeared exactly as it had before — and vanished just as it had then. Equally incredibly, his wife saw the same vision, just as clearly.

Jenkins's explanation is that the ghostly warriors may haunt the Cornish countryside and be made visible by psychic energy emanating from the nodes, or intersections, of the leys nearby. Loe Bar is located in a line that runs from Landewednack Church up through Breage Church and to a junction with two other leys at Townshend *(below)*.

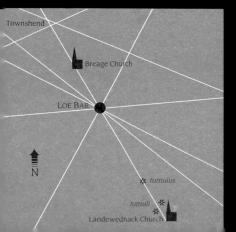

Levitation at Chanctonbury Ring

Chanctonbury Ring, an ancient earthwork circle crowned by a ring of beech trees, stands on a hilltop on the south coast of England. Once it was an Anglo-Saxon fort—thus, presumably, the scene of fierce battles. It stands at a nodal intersection of five leys, one going west past several tumuli to earthworks at Rackham Banks, another going north to Nun's Well, and three going east to Poynings Church, Devil's Dyke, and Kingston Church *(below)*.

On the night of August 25, 1974, a man named William Lincoln went to the site with three friends, all of them drawn by tales of any number of eerie occurrences there.

At about 11 p.m., as they entered the shadows of the ring of trees, Lincoln got more than he bargained for. Without warning, his companions later reported, he was snatched by an unseen force and lifted five feet into the air; he was suspended horizontally for thirty seconds or more before dropping back to the ground. Neither he nor his friends saw anything that could account for his levitation — but they got a memento of the occasion. One of Lincoln's companions, who had the presence of mind to take a tape recorder with him, came away with a tape on which Lincoln can be heard to shriek: ''No more! No more!'' in a plea to let him go.

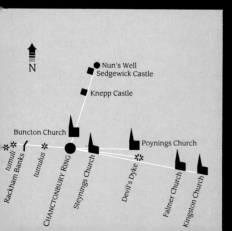

An Encounter on the Road to Chilcomb

Joyce Bowles, an employee of the Winchester Railway Station, was driving with her neighbor Ted Pratt to the nearby village of Chilcomb on a Sunday night in November 1976 to fetch her son Stephen. Suddenly, her car shook violently and careened onto the grass by the roadside. The headlights went out and the engine stopped. She and her passenger looked out the window, and both saw a cigar-shaped craft of glowing orange hovering above the road. Through its windows, they could see three heads lined up like passengers in a bus. Presently, one of the figures emerged from the craft and approached the car. He had piercing pink eyes without pupils or irises and was dressed in a silver jumpsuit. "He peered through the window at the dashboard controls," Joyce Bowles recalled. At that, the dead engine flared into life and the headlights went back on. "Then he and the cigar simply vanished," she said.

Some ley fanciers maintain that the lines hum with special terrestrial energies that attract unidentified aliens from space. Whatever the case, two alignments of ancient burial mounds that begin at Old Winchester Hill do indeed converge on Chilcomb Road (*below*), near the spot where Joyce Bowles and Ted Pratt said they experienced their peculiar encounter.

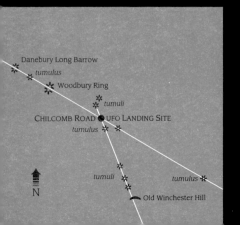

Danebury Long Barrow
tumulus
Woodbury Ring
tumuli
CHILCOMB ROAD • UFO LANDING SITE
tumulus

tumuli   *tumulus*

N
Old Winchester Hill

CHAPTER 4

Pictures on the Earth

tanding on the Nazca plateau in southern Peru one blazing afternoon in 1941, two Americans surveyed what seemed to be an immense, mystifying scratch pad of miles-long markings. Across the desert, hundreds of pale lines ran in every direction, crisscrossing each other in a chaotic tapestry. Some of the lines, known to the locals as Inca roads, radiated from a central point like wheel spokes or star bursts. Others connected with elongated triangles and trapezoids that looked startlingly like airport runways *(page 129).*

Historian Paul Kosok and his wife, Rose, had come to Peru to study ancient irrigation systems. But the bizarre markings in the Nazca desert (sometimes spelled Nasca), had inexorably drawn their attention. They decided to follow one of the wider lines in their truck; it led them up the steep side of a plateau and stopped in the midst of a widespread web of markings radiating from a central point on the plateau.

"We found not only many more lines," wrote Kosok later, "but also two huge rectangles or trapezoids. . . . Most amazing of all, we found adjacent to one of the rectangles and close to the original center, the faint remains of a huge, peculiar pebble and dirt drawing over 150 feet long.

"Finally, with our minds whirling with endless questions about these strange and fantastic remains, we returned to the center of radiation to view an impressive sunset. Just as we were watching the sun go down behind the horizon, we suddenly noticed that it was setting almost exactly over the end of one of the long single lines! A moment later we recalled that it was June 22, the day of the winter solstice in the Southern Hemisphere—the shortest day in the year and the day when the sun sets farthest north of due west. With a great thrill we realized at once that we had apparently found the key to the riddle."

Or had they? Kosok, in this flash of inspiration, concluded that the so-called Nazca lines formed a giant guide to the movement of the heavens—a notion derived from Sir J. Norman Lockyer's studies of Britain's Stonehenge earlier in the century *(page 91).* Yet Kosok's theory was soon disputed, taking its place as only one among many hotly debated ideas about the origins of the enigmatic Peruvian drawings. As word spread of the puzzle at Nazca, visiting archeologists found the riddle to be further complicated by the discovery of enormous animal figures carved on the desert floor and on adjoining hillsides: a wasp-waisted spider, a stylized hummingbird, a curiously pasturing owl-man presiding over the landscape. The giant drawings seemed to carry a message whose meaning had been lost in time.

Although the symbols on the Nazca desert form the most spectacular collection of geoglyphics—or earth drawings—in the world, they are not unique. Joining them in mystery are similar effigies—of snakes, birds, or humans—found on the mesas of the American Southwest and formed by the enigmatic sculptings of the ancient mound builders of the middle and southern United States. And in the southwestern region of England, there are hillside silhouettes of humans and horses, their origins lost in prehistory, which were carefully tended and maintained well into the modern era by local villagers who had little or no knowledge of the effigies' original purpose. By far the most puzzling aspect of these giant earthworks is that many of them cannot be seen in their entirety from the ground: Only from above do they begin to take on recognizable form. The riddle of why they were built and who was intended to view them has confounded archeologists and other investigators for years.

Of all the world's geoglyphics, none has attracted more attention—or stirred more controversy—than those at Nazca. Since Kosok's day, archeologists have mapped thousands of the lines, some stretching for five miles, and dozens of figures, including eighteen birds, ranging from twenty-seven to more than 450 feet long. They are scattered over approximately 500 square miles of an arid plateau between the western slope of the Andes and the Peruvian coast, where a fortuitous mix of geology and climate conspired to create an ideal medium for Nazca's earth artists.

Overlying the desert's base of yellow sand and clay is a thin layer of volcanic rocks and pebbles blackened from long exposure to the atmosphere. The lines on this so-called natural blackboard are little more than scratches in the surface, made by scraping away a few inches of rocks to expose the paler soil. In another climate, erosion would obliterate them within months. But Nazca is one of the driest regions on earth, averaging only about a half inch of rain every two years. Wind erosion is also minimal, thanks to a hot, still layer of air at ground level; this thermal buffer is formed by the dark-colored rocks, which absorb solar energy and radiate it as heat. Devoid of vegetation, Nazca's ageless tableau is so stark and otherworldly that observers have compared it to the surface of Mars.

Paul Kosok, in his brief tour around the area, became convinced that the lines might be part of an observatory for keeping track of celestial events. This would have allowed the ancient desert dwellers to calculate when the rivers would flow again, replenishing the aquifers and enabling them to plant their crops. But Kosok had to cut his Nazca investigations short and return to his teaching post at Long Island University in New York. Before leaving, though, he passed the mantle of chief detective on to a German-born acquaintance, Maria Reiche.

Kosok could not have chosen for himself a more dedicated disciple. Born in 1903 in the picturesque city of Dresden, Maria Reiche was the daughter of a judge. Myopic and shy, she was raised in a strict household that encouraged both her intellectual and her athletic abilities. By the 1920s, Reiche was excelling at mathematics and swimming at Hamburg University, and she had become an exceptionally independent and determined young woman.

The rise of the Nazi party convinced Reiche that she had to leave her homeland. In 1932, she saw an advertisement in a Hamburg newspaper for a job as governess for a wealthy German family living in Peru, and she jumped at the chance. By the end of the decade, she was working as a teacher and translating scientific papers in the capital city of Lima. It was there that she met Kosok, who, impressed by her mathematical and astronomical knowledge, challenged her to study the strange geoglyphics. Reiche, who was thirty-six years old at the time, would spend the rest of her life on the mystery of the lines. "I just slid into it," she once said in explaining her vocation. "I have always been very, very curious."

Giving up her job, Reiche moved from Lima to a town near Nazca in 1945 to devote all of her time to the lines, which she set about photographing and charting in exhaustive detail. A vegetarian and an ascetic, she lived in the desert for weeks on end, sleeping on a camp cot and subsisting on bread, cheese, fruit, and milk. At the time of the solstices, the wiry, bespectacled woman would rise before dawn and walk into the solitude of the plateau to watch the sun rise over the markings. Her observations supported those of Kosok: A number of lines pointed to the place of sunrise and sunset at the summer solstice and spring and fall equinoxes, as well as to spots on the horizon marking the seasonal appearance of major stars.

Reiche took a broom to the desert and methodically cleared the lines of debris. Indeed, she wore out such a quantity of brooms, purchased from a nearby town, that at first the local inhabitants feared she was a witch. Once, after walking in circles for days, sweeping clear a spiraling path, Reiche suddenly realized that she was standing on the tail of a gigantic monkey figure. "I just sat down on the pampa and laughed," she recalled later. Uncovering more of the huge, stylized animal symbols, she noted their similarity to the figures on the pottery and textiles of the Nazca Indians. Archeologists who began to visit the site confirmed her suspicions; artifacts found near the lines date to the era when the Nazca Indian culture dominated the desert.

Little is known of these early, coastal Peruvians, who seem to have had a complex society long before the Inca Empire. It appears that they lived by farming, employing a sophisticated irrigation system, and that they built pyramids and created brilliant pottery and textiles. Thousands of shards of colorful ceramics, most from the Nazca culture—approximately 300 B.C. to A.D. 540—litter the Nazca plateau. These fragments—and the mysterious lines—are virtually the only legacy of the inhabitants of that desert.

As a mathematician, Reiche was intrigued by the possibility that the Nazcas may have relied on geometric principles in the design and construction of their markings. She found that the straightness of the lines, many of which run for many miles over hills and gullies without ever veering from true, was probably achieved by stringing a cord between wooden posts and using it as a guide; keeping three posts always in a line of sight assured that the overall line remained straight.

While straight lines would have been relatively simple to execute, the curved lines characteristic of the animal figures were much more complicated. Reiche decided that the curves were actually a series of linked arcs, each representing a small section of the circumference of a different circle. Each arc could have been created by securing one end of a cord and sweeping the other end across the ground like a compass. Reiche claimed to have found the centers of some of these circles in the form of small areas where the rocks had been disturbed. She proposed, too, that the radii of the various circles were part of a mathematical code that, if deciphered,

Steadied by two assistants, Maria Reiche surveys the vast Nazca designs traced in the Peruvian desert. The teacher spent more than four decades mapping and analyzing the ancient figures.

would reveal a key to the movement of the stars and planets.

Reiche's investigations also revealed that the Nazcas worked out their designs in advance on smaller plots about six feet square. She found evidence of these dirt sketch pads beside several of the larger figures. Once the designers had established the proper relationship among arcs, center points, and radii for a figure on the small preliminary drawing, they could then plot them on the larger scale.

Finally, by carefully comparing proportions between figures and their components, Reiche determined that the designers used several units of measure. The drawings could be divided evenly into Nazcan "feet" of about ten inches and "yards" measuring about four and a half feet. Another unit that appears with some regularity includes one just under six feet (5.95 feet). When she measured a giant trident-shaped geoglyphic known as the Candelabra, located on a hillside at Pisco Bay some 130 miles north of Nazca, she found it to be, suggestively, 595 feet long. Scholars continue to debate the origins of this spectacular drawing.

Reiche's life revolved around the changeless desert and its people. Over time, the wispy figure in the simple cotton dress, alpaca socks, and rubber thong sandals became a Peruvian hero: The town of Nazca celebrates her birthday and has named a school and a street in her honor. She has also gained international recognition for her single-minded study of *las líneas*. The "very, very curious" woman was still at it well into the 1980s—a frail, half-blind octogenarian obsessed with the secrets of the ancient Nazcas.

Despite her exhaustive work, Maria Reiche did not win universal acceptance for her theories about the purpose and construction of the lines. Some observers, feeling that there must be more to the mysterious drawings than astronomy, proposed more exotic solutions. One such theorist was a former Swiss hotelier and fledgling author named Erich von Däniken.

Born in Zofingen, Switzerland, in 1935, von Däniken was an inveterate individualist who revolted early against his stern father and the Roman Catholic Church in which he was raised. Astronomy, archeology, and the study of unidentified

The Candelabra of the Andes is etched into a mountainside overlooking the Pacific Ocean. Not much is known of the 595-foot-long figure; various theorists have called it a symbol of the Trinity, a depiction of the tree of life, and a signpost for ancient astronauts.

flying objects appealed to him far more than did the subjects taught in school.

His rebellious nature showed itself in other ways as well. At the age of nineteen, von Däniken was convicted of stealing from a camp where he worked as a youth leader. Shortly afterward, he became apprenticed to an innkeeper but soon fled this workaday existence for Egypt, a country better suited to his restless, romantic spirit. When he returned to Switzerland, his involvement in an alleged jewelry scam finally caught up with him; he was convicted for embezzlement and sentenced to a nine-month jail term.

After his release, the energetic von Däniken took a job as a cook and waiter in a hotel in Davos, Switzerland, where he soon worked his way up to manager. With his life seemingly in order, he began traveling around the world to gather evidence for his developing theories about the origins of enigmas such as the Great Pyramid of Cheops and the geoglyphics at Nazca. Back in Switzerland, he tended to his guests during the day, then toiled long into the night on the manuscript that would become his first book, *Chariots of the Gods?*

In this extraordinary and controversial work, von Däniken proposed that the Nazca lines were intended as runways for alien spaceships. Extraterrestrial astronauts, the author declared, landed at Nazca as well as at other locations in the ancient world. Visiting many times over thousands of years, they profoundly influenced human destiny by interbreeding with our remote ancestors, imparting to them the genes for superior intelligence. Furthermore, the extraterrestrials left their calling cards in such diverse forms as the Nazca lines, carvings in Mayan temples, the pyramids of Egypt, a mysterious metal column in India, and the cave drawings of prehistoric cultures in Russia and China. As further evidence for his claims, von Däniken cited visitation myths from ancient religions as well as various references from the Bible, including the prophet Ezekiel's vision of "wheels of fire"—in reality, von Däniken proposed, flying saucers.

Von Däniken's scenario for Nazca called for "unknown intelligences" landing there in the distant past and building a pair of runways for their spacecraft. After completing their earthly mission and returning home, von Däniken would explain in *Gods from Outer Space,* a sequel to *Chariots of the Gods?,* "the pre-Inca tribes, who had observed these beings at work and been tremendously impressed by them, longed passionately for the return of these 'gods.' They waited for years and when their wish was not fulfilled, they began to make new lines on the plain, just as they had seen the 'gods' make them." The animal figures came later, as the Nazcas gradually forgot the true purpose of the markings.

Von Däniken had hoped his book would be a ticket to freedom after the humdrum life of hotel management—and so it was. After rejection by a dozen publishers, *Chariots of the Gods?* was finally accepted, and it became an international bestseller as soon as it hit the stores in 1968. That year may have been the best and worst of von Däniken's life. The newly celebrated author became—for the second time—a convicted embezzler, sentenced to a year in prison for cheating his hotel out of $130,000 to finance his research junkets.

Not surprisingly, most scientists dismissed von Däniken's dramatic thesis out of hand. In the view of his detractors, von Däniken's notion that the lines resulted from a visit by extraterrestrials simply failed to jibe with common sense. "It is hard to believe," wrote scholar E. C. Krupp, "that visiting spacemen, who must have the technological capacity to travel hundreds of light-years to earth, would require either landing strips or gigantic navigational markers once they arrived." And as Maria Reiche pointed out, Nazca's soft, sandy soil is unsuitable for the landing of heavy aircraft. "I'm afraid the spacemen would have gotten stuck," she said.

The critics were no gentler with von Däniken himself, describing him as an intellectual con man whose work was characterized by "a dearth of supporting data, an endless stream of false and misleading information, a sprinkling of truth, and some of the most illogical reasoning ever to appear in print." The author, who has admitted that some of the material was mistaken or not meant to be taken seriously, replied cheerfully, "I'm the only author who has really frightened the critics. Other writers sit at home and wait for miracles. 'I'm *making* the miracles!'"

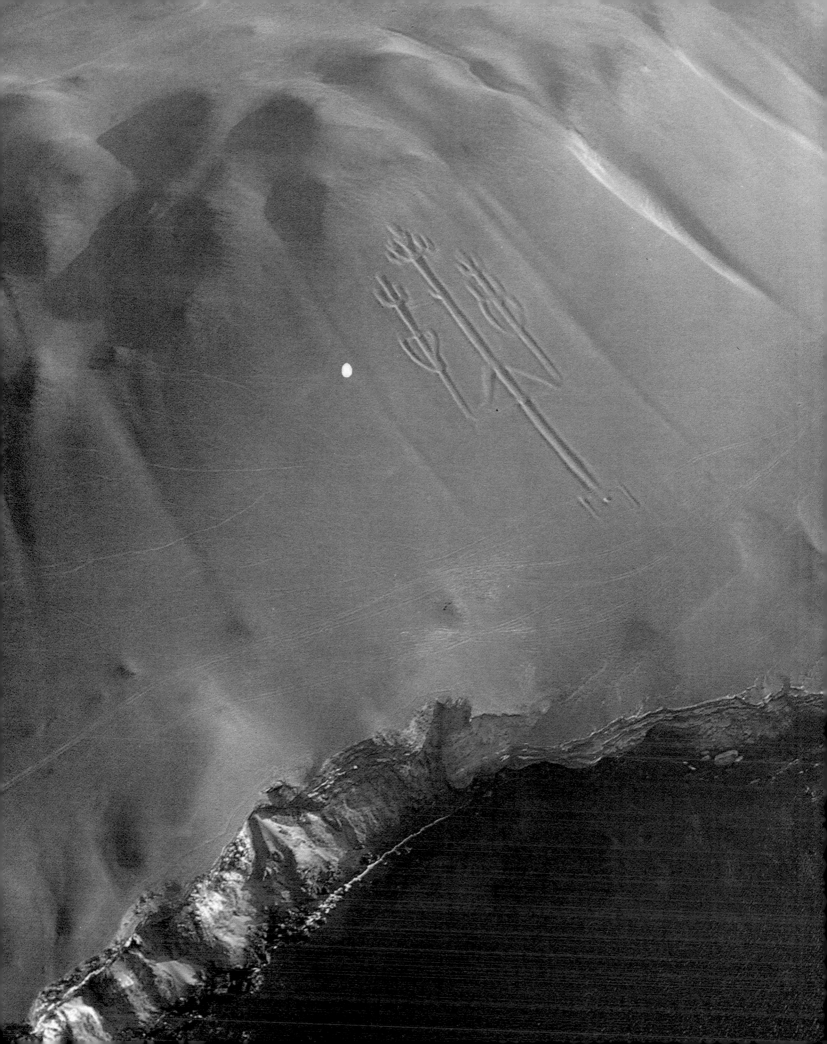

Author Erich von Däniken claims that this Mexican sarcophagus lid commemorates an alien visitor. Experts say the relief depicts a Mayan nobleman's death.

Regardless of whether he is guilty or innocent, or whatever his degree of integrity as a writer, there is no question that von Däniken was able to reach a vast audience of people who enthusiastically believe human history contains secrets beyond the limits of conventional archeology or traditional science. His books drew praise from a large and fanatically loyal readership: Less than a decade after the publication of *Chariots of the Gods?* von Däniken's works boasted international total sales approaching 34 million copies. Von Däniken's central thesis—that the lines on the Nazca desert were meant to be seen from the air and could thus have been directed only to ancient astronauts—was put to the test when an American reader, airline executive Jim Woodman, visited the area in the fall of 1973. At the age of forty, the boyish, tousle-haired businessman had already founded Air Florida and become a member of the Miami-based International Explorers Society when he decided to take a closer look at lines he had glimpsed on earlier trips. Woodman was flabbergasted by the ''colossal puzzle'' he saw below him when he flew in a small airplane over the Nazca desert. Later, as he

turned the riddle of the lines over in his mind, the conclusion grew on him—just as it had on von Däniken—that the creators of this panorama must have intended it to be viewed from the air. However, Woodman dismissed any idea that the lines were intended for the eyes of extraterrestrials. Instead, he decided, they were probably meant to be seen by the Nazcas themselves. But how?

The first piece of the puzzle fell into place when a friend, fledgling balloonist Bill Spohrer, offhandedly suggested that perhaps the Nazcas flew in lighter-than-air craft. Woodman seized this improbable notion and began to collect supporting evidence. The information he uncovered surprised and delighted him. For instance, the Incas, successors to the Nazcas in the Peruvian hills, had several legends about characters who could fly. Woodman also discovered the suggestive account of a Brazilian priest, Bartolomeu de Gusmão, who in 1709 supposedly flew a model hot-air balloon before the Portuguese court in Lisbon. From Woodman's perspective, the important part of Gusmão's story was his background: He was born and raised in Brazil and could well have been inspired by accounts of Indian balloons brought back by explorers from the South American frontier. Furthermore, Woodman claimed that images of flight—including symbols resembling balloons or kites and soaring, birdlike men—decorate many pieces of Nazca pottery and textiles.

The more he thought about it, the more convinced Woodman became that the Nazcas knew the secret of flight and regularly floated aloft in balloons. He came to believe that the Indians staged religious ceremonies associated with their balloon flights on the so-called runways and launched the balloons with smoke created in nearby burn pits, remnants of which survive as groupings of charred-looking rocks within the lines. Filled with excitement, Woodman set out to prove his daring thesis through a kind of experimental archeology: He decided to build his own Nazca-style hot-air balloon and actually fly in it. Only one name for the balloon would do—it would be called *Condor I,* after the giant soaring bird of the Andes.

Woodman knew that for the sake of credibility he would have to build *Condor I* with materials and methods as close to the Nazcas' as possible. For the balloon's envelope, or air bag, he chose a modern cotton fabric whose weave and weight were nearly identical to cloth samples from Nazca burial shrouds. For the shape of the envelope, he relied on descriptions of Gusmão's balloon and on his interpretation of flight images on Nazca textiles and pottery. The South Dakota firm that built *Condor I* stitched the envelope in the form of a tetrahedron—an inverted pyramid open at the bottom to let in smoke. The banana-shaped gondola was woven from totora reeds harvested along the shores of Lake Titicaca, high on the Peru-Bolivia border.

By the end of November 1975, *Condor I*—eighty-eight feet high and blazoned with designs based on scenes from the Nazca desert—was ready for its maiden flight. Woodman and his team of thirty, which included British ballooning champion Julian Nott as copilot and seventy-two-year-old Maria Reiche as an observer, assembled on the Nazca desert and went to work.

First, the balloonists built a burn pit to generate the hot smoke needed for lift-off. The pit included a fire hole filled with wood and connected by a twenty-five-foot covered trench to a smoke pit, over which the mouth of *Condor I's* envelope was secured. Next, the envelope had to be "cured" to render its weave airtight. To accomplish this, Woodman's crew pumped smoke into the envelope over several days until the tiny gaps in the weave were plugged with soot.

The balloon fully cured, Woodman was ready at last to fulfill his dream. In their decidedly non-Nazca flight uniforms of crash helmets and Navy coveralls, he and copilot Nott boarded *Condor I* at 5:30 in the morning. The mooring lines were slipped, and with astonishing speed the two aeronauts climbed silently into the dawn sky. Within seconds they floated to nearly 400 feet above the desert.

"The sun had just cleared the mountains," wrote Woodman later, "and now flooded the fantastic scene below. As we hung there drifting slightly to the northwest, I was astonished to see a long Nasca runway perhaps 300 yards off our starboard side. . . . The great plains ran to the horizon and several ancient lines stood out clearly in the morning sun.

Surely, I thought, the men who created these lines had to have seen them like this—with the shadows of dawn etching their magnificent art."

After three minutes, the balloon began descending as the air in the envelope cooled. When the craft reached the ground and the two crewmen hopped from the gondola, the suddenly lightened Condor I shot into the air again to an altitude of 1,200 feet and sailed several miles before gradually sinking to the desert for the second and final time. It had flown for a total of fourteen minutes—long enough, as far as Woodman was concerned, to prove his point that the Nazcas could indeed have taken to the sky in a hot-air balloon.

The theories of Woodman, von Däniken, and Reiche notwithstanding, Nazca remains an enigma. Each solution to the mystery seemed to raise more questions. Woodman's experiment with Condor I demonstrated that the Nazcas had the materials for building hot-air balloons: But in the absence of hard evidence, his theory that they actually flew in them was fascinating speculation at best.

Kosok's theory that Nazca was a giant observatory also has been criticized. In 1968, astronomer Gerald Hawkins visited the desert, where he plotted the lines in order to analyze, by computer, their relationship with various heavenly bodies. Hawkins had applied the same technique in 1963 to deduce an astronomical key to Stonehenge (page 92). The astronomer picked out ninety-three linear features and ran a program to match them with positions of the sun, moon, the Pleiades star cluster, and the forty-five brightest stars in the sky. After tracking the correlations for each century from 5000 B.C. to the present, Hawkins found, surprisingly, no significant overall match between the lines and the sky: "Astronomically speaking," he wrote, "the system is random."

The Nazca desert's inscrutability did nothing to stem the flow of imaginative theories. Researchers have suggested that the lines were used for choreography, or as tracks for foot races, or for laying out threads for weaving. A sculptor proposed that the animal figures might be prescient examples of modern minimalist art. In what might be thought of as a birth control theory, scholar William Isbell asserted that the act of constructing the lines, by employing a large labor force, served as a check on the Nazca population and prevented it from outgrowing its resource-poor environment.

And yet, for want of evidence, none of these proposals has satisfied the Nazca detectives. New explanations continued to surface in the 1970s and 1980s. Several were based on the known religious customs of both the Incas and the Indian populations still populating the Andean altiplano in Peru, Bolivia, and Chile. For instance, U.S. scholar Johan Reinhard suggested in 1985 that the lines and figures were linked to a form of mountain worship. According to this theory, the Nazcas associated the distant Andes with rain and fertility—a reasonable assumption, since the intermittent rivers that flowed onto the desert came from the mountains. A number of the drawings at Nazca—including a cormorant, a frog, a duck, and a killer whale—are of water animals and are associated with rain or fertility in Andean culture today.

Several investigators, including British explorer and writer Tony Morrison, University of Illinois anthropologist Tom Zuidema, and Colgate University anthropologists Anthony Aveni and Gary Urton, see an intriguing parallel between the spokelike lines emanating from "ray centers" and similar motifs found in other areas of the Andes. Andean Indians today follow the Inca tradition of walking along lines, or ceques, such as those at Nazca for various spiritual as well as practical purposes. According to some authorities, each Nazca kinship group or extended family might have had its own ray center and set of lines, with the more extensive sets accorded to groups higher up on the social scale.

Like so many other theories, the ceques proposal stops short of proof; the Nazca drawings seem almost to resist final answers. Equally stubborn in their mystery are the myriad other such figures that pepper the globe, some of them in places hardly less obscure than the Peruvian desert.

In 1923, some 3,000 miles to the north of Nazca, Colonel Jerry Phillips of the United States Army Air Service was flying an open-cockpit World War I biplane 5,000 feet over the Mojave

A Wheel to Watch the Heavens

High in the Bighorn Mountains of Wyoming, on the stony surface of a windswept plateau, lies the ghostly outline of a spoked wheel eighty-two feet in diameter. Similar rocky circles appear in Saskatchewan, in Arizona, and at some fifty other sites across the North American plains. Some are a few feet in diameter, others are hundreds of times as large. All lie on high ground.

The wheels are built simply: Thin ridges of stones form a rim, hub, and usually a number of spokes. Some have rocky piles, called cairns, in their centers and around the outer circles. The Bighorn medicine wheel — so-called because, to the American Indian, any object with spiritual properties was said to have medicine — is the best preserved and best known.

Historians guess that Plains Indians made this circle as early as the 1100s, but they cannot be certain. Nor do investigators know the exact purpose of any of the wheels — though clues may lie in their orientation.

At the Bighorn wheel, for instance, an observer who sights over the cairn in the foreground *(above)* toward the hub will look into the rising sun on the morning of the summer solstice. A second cairn would mark sunset on the same day. Other rock piles point to the rising and setting of three brilliant stars during seasonal changes.

Such alignments lead some theorists to believe that the medicine wheels, like their huge megalithic cousins in Europe, were in fact astronomical observatories. This contention is strengthened by the fact that all such wheels are carefully positioned to offer clear views of the horizon. Furthermore, cairns in some wheels cover postholes that may have held upright timbers, so that the original sites would have looked almost like wooden versions of Stonehenge in England.

But critical questions remain. Why would Plains Indians need to watch the sky? Agricultural tribes might have wanted to keep track of growing seasons, but the nomadic Plains peoples lived by hunting bison. Could they have remembered an earlier age when they planted crops? Or did the solstice mark the turning point of the summer for them, a time to begin counting the days until the start of their southward migration?

Such questions may never be answered. Like the builders of so many of the earth's markings, those who laid out the medicine wheels have vanished, leaving later generations no key to their strange monuments.

Desert. Near the small town of Blythe, California, he happened to glance down at the arid landscape. "I could hardly believe what I saw," he said later. Sprawled across the desert, far from civilization, were the gigantic figures of a man and a long-tailed animal.

Reports of the so-called Blythe Giant continued in the decades to come, prompting scientists and other investigators to take a closer look at the little-known southwestern desert. There, along the arid lower valley of the Colorado River, they have discovered some 275 geoglyphics, obscure symbols, and bizarre, childlike drawings of humans and animals. The Mojave's surface, like that of the Nazca desert, is covered with rocks varnished to a dark sheen by the sun; apparently the Mojave artists used the same rock-removal technique as the Nazcas to create their enigmatic messages.

Most of these desert markings have been discovered since the 1970s, thanks to the tireless efforts of California archeologist Jay von Werlhof and his collaborator, a local farmer and pilot named Harry Casey. By plane and foot, they have reconnoitered thousands of square miles of the blistering ground that early Spanish explorers called *tierra del muerto,* "land of the dead." The collaborators' goal is to catalogue and describe every desert marking in this vast region. "It's absolutely addictive," Casey has said of his quest. "The more you learn, the more you want to know."

Von Werlhof and his fellow archeologists believe the figures found on the Mojave were created for mystic purposes by the Indians who have inhabited the desert for more than 5,000 years. They date the oldest of the figures to 3000 B.C. and the most recent of them to the late eighteenth century A.D. More primitive configurations, known as rock alignments—twisting lines of boulders set side by side in abstract patterns—may be as much as 10,000 years old.

The investigators offer several interpretations of the weird tableau at Blythe, whose age is variously estimated at between 200 and 1,000 years. According to legends passed down by the Mojave Indians, the manlike form represents an evil giant who terrorized their ancestors. The animal figure, which seems to float upside down over the man's head, is said to be a mountain lion imbued with great power from the Mojave's creator god; it was placed there to weaken the giant's spirit. A less dramatic theory suggests that the giant is a kind of graphic "no trespassing" sign placed by Hopi Indians to keep intruders out of their territory.

Many of the animal figures seem to have retained a spiritual significance to the desert dwellers. A 180-foot-long rattlesnake with basalt eyes, according to Mojave medicine men, has powers of good or evil that can be passed on to humans. A figure near Yuma, Arizona, is clearly that of a horse, an animal unknown to the southwestern Indians before the coming of Europeans. Archeologists believe that the Indians created the image sometime after Spanish explorers rode through the area in 1540 and that they subsequently used the desert drawing as a ceremonial meeting place. Another figure, not discovered until July 1984, is a startlingly animated rendering of a fisherman who appears to be dancing on water while aiming a spear at two fish. The tip of the spear is made of hundreds of pieces of glittering quartz and may have been designed to bestow magic powers on real fishermen.

Like their counterparts at Nazca, the Mojave figures apparently served a variety of purposes, and at least some of the drawings may have been astronomical markers. A rock alignment along the Gila River in Arizona, for example, points precisely to the sunrise at summer solstice. Another, known as the Black Point Dance Circle, may have been designed as a map of the sun, moon, and Milky Way. Knowledge of the heavens could have given Indians a calendar with which to plan their farming and irrigation—vital information in a difficult environment.

Whatever the purpose of their elaborately drawn geoglyphics, the Indians of the Nazca and Mojave deserts were blessed with ideal natural blackboards upon which to scratch out their designs. The natives of the temperate forests of the American Midwest and South were not so fortunate, but they still managed to mark the landscape with impressive animal figures. Like their desert counterparts, these images can best be appreciated from the air; unlike the others, however, they are also easily visible from the ground, rising from the earth in great sculptured masses.

Pioneers entering the Ohio valley in the 1780s were perplexed by the presence of large and obviously man-made mounds. They were even more amazed to discover that some were in the shape of animals—the most spectacular example being a sinuous, quarter-mile-long serpent writhing along the top of a ridge near the modern-day town of Peebles, Ohio. Effigy mounds were also found throughout the Mississippi valley and in other regions of the eastern United States. A further surprise was in store along the shores of the Mississippi River, where explorers found, near the present-day site of East St. Louis, Illinois, a huge, truncated pile of earth resembling the base of an Egyptian pyramid.

Awed by the size of the earthworks and mindful of the effort it must have taken to construct them, the white settlers speculated about their builders. It seemed unlikely that ancestors of the simple woodland Indians who inhabited the region could have built such imposing structures. Instead, observers agreed that the mounds were products of some vanished, noble race whose civilization had been destroyed by invading tribes in the same way that Rome was laid waste by barbarians. Therefore, according to the numerous variations on this theme, the mounds must have been constructed by descendants of the survivors of the Flood, or by migrants from the lost continent of Atlantis, or by the lost tribes of Israel that were mentioned in the Old Testament. Or else they were monuments erected by shepherds from India, by a race of giants, or by Greeks, Romans, Egyptians, Phoenicians, or Danes who in the distant past had somehow wandered onto the North American continent.

The mysterious effigies attracted many amateurs in the budding science of American archeology. One of the most colorful of these enthusiasts was William Pidgeon, an itinerant trader and collector of Indian artifacts. Thin, bespectacled, and severe-looking, Pidgeon was in fact a classic nineteenth-century romantic, devoted to discovering the lost secrets of the noble races he believed had once inhabited the Americas. His passion for archeology took him throughout North and South America, and he claimed to have a detailed knowledge of Indian cultures on both continents. In the 1830s, he settled at a place called Fort Ancient, overlooking Ohio's Little Miami River. The fort was actually a large mound—another of what Pidgeon regarded as the "stupendous and wonderful" remnants of a lost civilization. In a quest to learn more about these remarkable earthworks, the trader built a small boat and set out in 1840 along the network of streams and lakes west of the Great Lakes.

He was astonished by what he found. The woods were populated with menageries of animal effigies—earth mounds in the shape of panthers, lizards, turtles, falcons, and, on a ridge in Iowa, what appeared to be an entire family of bears marching in single file. At the trading settlement of Prairie La Crosse on the upper Mississippi, Pidgeon later reported, he met De-coo-dah, a medicine man who immediately warmed to this eccentric paleface with his insatiable curiosity about Indian ways. The old man took Pidgeon under his wing and began instructing him in tribal lore. On one point he was abundantly clear: When the country was inhabited by his early ancestors, game was plentiful and afforded them the leisure to build the earth sculptures. "The face of the earth is the red man's book," he declared, "and those mounds and embankments are some of his letters." Pidgeon said he impressed the medicine man by throwing his trowel into the river, vowing never again to desecrate the places of his red brethren. But he ignored the main point, sticking with the prevalent notion that the mounds could only have been built by some "superior" race.

Pidgeon may have been closer to the mark in some of his other calculations, however. For example, he accepted De-coo-dah's explanation that serpent effigies such as the gigantic snake at Peebles, Ohio, were astronomical in character. As his Indian mentor explained, when "the worshippers of reptiles were reduced by the fortunes of war, and compelled to recognize the sun, moon, and heavenly bodies as the only objects worthy of adoration, they secretly entombed their gods in the earth-work symbols which represented the heavenly bodies."

Not until the late nineteenth century did people finally concede that the mound builders and the living Indians were of the same race. In the 1880s, a government ethnologist named Cyrus Thomas surveyed more than 2,000 Indian sites across the eastern and midwestern United States. His thorough fieldwork, backed by exhaustive archival research, produced the first comprehensive study of North American Indians. Based on tribal legends, the accounts of early explorers, and physical examination of more than 4,000 artifacts, Thomas's assertion of Indian descent from the mound builders could no longer be disputed.

Archeologists divide these mound builders into three broad cultures: Adena, Hopewell, and Mississippian. Named after a mound site in Ohio, the Adena culture was centered in the upper Midwest and existed between 1000 B.C. and A.D. 200. Its people built burial mounds and animal effigies; the best known is the awesome Great Serpent Mound of Ohio.

The Hopewell culture, which overlapped and eventually replaced the Adena, flourished between 200 B.C. and A.D. 550— about the same period as the Nazcas. Skilled artisans and traders, the Hopewells and their immediate successors built most of the great earth effigies and fortlike structures that so amazed Pidgeon and other early archeologists.

The last and greatest of the mound-building cultures was the Mississippian, which began about A.D. 600 and dominated aboriginal society for the next thousand years. Its achievements were best represented by Cahokia, a major pre-Columbian metropolis at the present site of East St. Louis and the home of the strange pyramid that had amazed early explorers. Mississippian society was by far the most elaborate and structured of the three cultures and its edifices the largest.

The Mississippians were unfortunate enough to witness the arrival of whites in the person of Hernando de Soto and his conquistadors, who crossed what is now the southeastern United States in 1539. The Spaniards left a trail of death and destruction in their wake; within a generation of their passage, the region's Indian population had been decimated by smallpox and other diseases. Their culture then faded away.

A central mystery remains: We may know who built the mounds, but we do not know why. Some 150 years after Decoo-dah told William Pidgeon about the link between mounds and constellations, scientists have no better explanation. Indirect evidence, at least, supports the old Indian's story. For instance, psychologist Thaddeus M. Cowan of Kansas University has noted that Ohio's Great Serpent Mound may follow a worldwide cultural tradition in which snakes symbolize celestial events. The traditional image of a lunar eclipse in Asia, for example, is a snake swallowing an egg—the very act depicted by the Ohio effigy. Cowan proposed that the snake represents the Little Dipper, a constellation whose handle ends at Polaris, the North Star. The evidence is intriguing: The turns in the snake's body correspond to the stars in the handle, while the snake's tail spirals in the same clockwise direction as the Little Dipper's rotation around Polaris. Using the same criteria, Cowan links other effigies of birds and bears to the Big Dipper and the Northern Cross.

But such theories are guesswork. Time and change have silenced the mound builders forever. However, their spirits may still remain. In 1975, a curious and literally hair-raising incident took place at Ohio's Great Serpent Mound, which suggests to some people that these cultures left behind more than their massive monuments.

Sociologist Robert W. Harner was driving through the state one warm November afternoon when he decided, on a whim, to see the mound he had first visited as a child. He stood alone on the serpent's head that windless day, he recalled later, wondering why the builders had chosen that inconvenient hill for their sculpture. Then, suddenly, he felt an overwhelming sense of dread—"the coldest, most abject, hopeless terror I have ever experienced. I felt the hair rising on the nape of my neck; I could neither move nor speak. I knew that although I was completely alone, I was not really alone." Frozen with fear, Harner said he could only watch as the leaves below him, first one by one and then in small groups, gathered themselves up and began to move toward him up the ridge. Still there was no wind; yet the leaves crept unnaturally toward him, rising and falling like footfalls. When they were fifteen or twenty feet away, they flew togeth-

The most famous of America's earthen mounds, Ohio's Great Serpent, uncoils across a thousand feet to gra

sphere in its mouth. According to one legend, Indians fashioned the snake to commemorate a lunar eclipse.

er, swirling around him in a macabre dance. Harner forced himself to break away, turning toward his car for a camera, but at that instant the spell was broken. "I saw that already the leaves were walking back down the hillside and I knew I never could get back in time to photograph them."

As a shaken Harner contemplated the incident, he was certain he had glimpsed some "small portion of that world I did not believe existed," a spirit world the builders of the Great Serpent may have known, too. "Perhaps," he concluded, "they built their mound on that particular hill because very special things happen there."

If there is a spirit world, and if its inhabitants are drawn to these great symbols on the earth, these spirits may also feel at home in the emerald hills of southwest England. For there, as well as in other parts of Britain, huge figures of humans and beasts loom on the green hillsides, Old World counterparts of the enigmas at Nazca and Ohio. Created by removing sod from the hills to expose the bright limestone bedrock a few feet below, the British figures show a single-minded concentration on two symbols: horses and humans. Archeologists believe that prehistoric Britain boasted many such earth effigies, most of which were long ago reclaimed by vegetation. Several of them, however, have been preserved over the centuries; historical accounts and old coins found nearby have led some scientists to believe that at least two of the figures—the White Horse of Uffington and the Cerne Giant—may well date from the beginning of the Christian Era, when Britain was ruled by pagan Celtic tribes.

Named for a Berkshire village and located about sixty-five miles west of London, the Uffington Horse gallops sleekly along the ridge of a 500-foot hill *(page 136)*. As long as a football field, this stylized steed flows across the landscape—it is a wonderfully dynamic piece of early art.

Like several other British effigies, the Uffington Horse lies close to an ancient hilltop fort; some scholars speculate that the image served as a tribal emblem for frightening enemies. A more intriguing possibility, however, is suggested by its association with Dragon Hill, a flattened summit immediately to the north. There, legend has it, England's patron saint, George, slew a dragon. (The legend also states that, to this day, no grass will grow on the spot where the dragon's blood spilled.) In the view of some archeologists, when the west-country Celts converted to Christianity, they may have substituted Saint George for an earlier pagan demigod associated with horses. It is even possible that the horse itself was originally meant to be a dragon; scholars point to its beaklike jaw, recalling an earlier reptilian form. Seventy miles away, across a hillside in Dorsetshire, lies the 180-foot-tall Cerne Giant *(page 137)*. This figure, brandishing a huge club, was known for centuries as the Rude Man of Cerne because of his conspicuous nudity. Like the Uffington Horse, the figure is a mystery. Some scholars associate the giant with a Hercules cult that flourished around the Roman emperor Commodus in the second century A.D., while others believe the behemoth is a rendering of the Celtic god Nodens. Folklore claims that the figure represents a huge Dane who was killed and beheaded there. Yet another theory holds that the giant was the center of a pagan fertility cult, one that continued—in the watered-down form of a Maypole dance—long after Britain was Christianized in the seventh century.

Whatever its role, the Cerne Giant and other hillside figures loomed large in the lives of the local people, linking them with the land and a long spiritual tradition. Accounts dating back to the seventeenth century record that every seven years on Whitsunday, the seventh Sunday after Easter, Uffington villagers would gather to restore the great white horse by scything away the accumulated vegetation. A festival with much drinking and merrymaking followed long into the night. The last of these pastimes, as they were called, was in 1857.

Other depictions of huge horses and giants stride across the chalky hills of England; unlike the Uffington Horse or the Cerne Giant, no mystery surrounds their origins or purpose. All but a few derive from the eighteenth and nineteenth centuries and were created by local gentry for the purpose of decorating the landscape. In drawing on the earth, however, landowners were following a tradition thousands of years old, a deep-rooted compulsion to leave their mark.

Britain's ancient hill figures, America's earth effigies, Nazca's inscrutable chaos of lines—all speak across the centuries, challenging professional scholars and enthusiastic amateurs to plumb their secrets. Despite some plausible theories, the gulf of time and culture is so great that, as Maria Reiche has said of the Nazca desert's *líneas*, "we will never know all the answers." In the face of phenomena so strange and complex, the most dedicated students remain humble.

Artifacts from Indian mounds add to the mystery of America's early peoples. The sandstone disk below, unearthed in Alabama, may have been used in warfare rituals. Even less is known of the six-inch cat found in Florida (opposite).

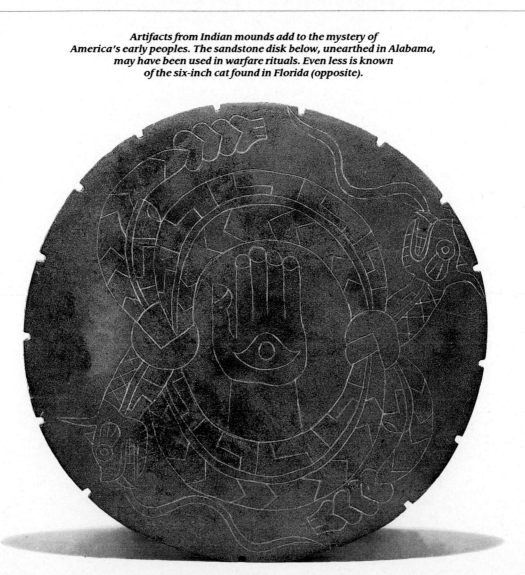

Glyphs for the Gods

When the Wright brothers lofted their tiny biplane over the sands of Kitty Hawk, North Carolina, in 1903, they opened up not only the heavens but the earth as well. Early aviators found to their delight that flight transformed a familiar world, giving it mysterious new shapes and textures. And as aviation progressed through the 1920s and 1930s, pilots who patrolled the airways of Peru or the American Southwest or England's rolling hills began to see wonders. Giant works of art — huge geometric figures, owl-eyed humans, enormous galloping horses — sprang out of the anonymous landscape with surprising vividness. Some seemed to stare almost imploringly at the sky, as if seeking the eyes of gods.

And therein lies their mystery. We may never know why or for whom the ground dwellers of the Nazca plateau or Britain's hills created these earth drawings. But through the modern magic of aerial photography, we can see the images as perhaps they were meant to be seen — from the air.

American photographer Marilyn Bridges is a master of this art. Captivated by the experience of photographing Nazca lines of Peru in the late 1970s, she went on to shoot many of the world's most famous earth drawings from the sky. Her methods are hair-raising: Hugging the land at what a friend calls "a witch's distance" of 200 feet, their wings banked at a fifty-degree angle to gain the best perspective, her airplanes often cruise so slowly as to risk stalling. Bridges prefers to work in the early morning or late afternoon light, with its long, dramatic shadows; similarly, she uses black-and-white film to best bring out the contrasting forms of nature and art. The following pages contain a sampling of her images.

The arrowlike half-mile-long Great Triangle is sometimes called a runway for alien spaceships. But most believe that it was an astronomical marker or a ritual gathering place.

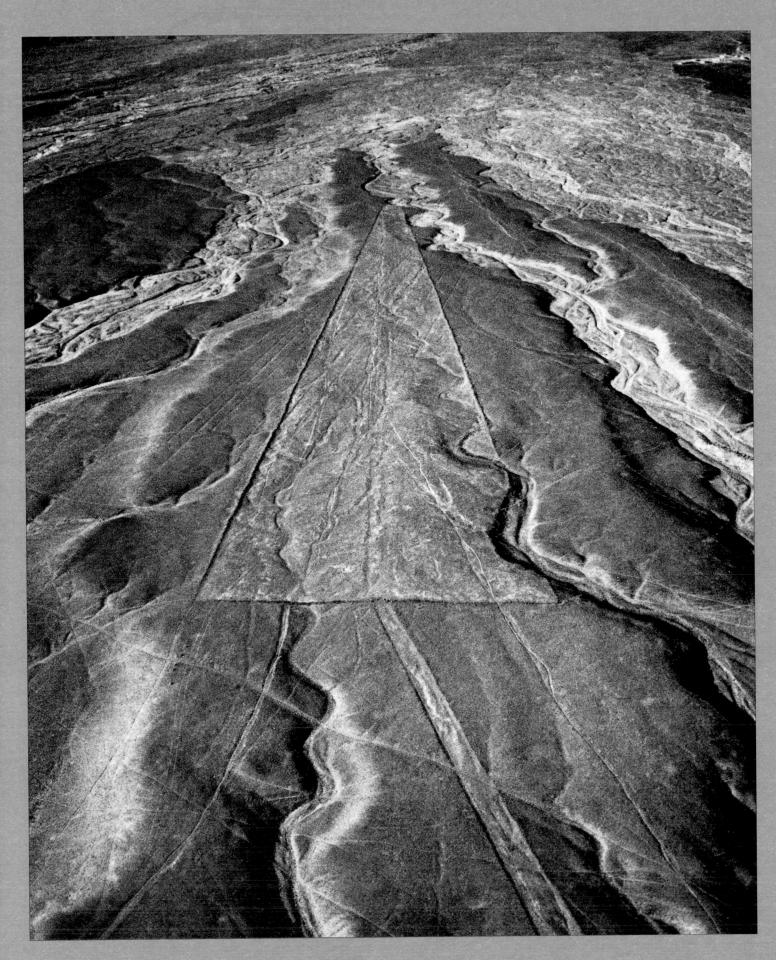

A stylized hummingbird is one of eighteen bird figures carved on the Nazca plateau. Such drawings may have symbolized seasonal changes: This creature's 120-foot beak ends at a line that marks sunrise at the winter solstice.

*Scarred by automobile tracks, an anatomically
accurate Nazcan spider spans 150 feet of desert. Like most of the Peruvian drawings,
it is formed by one continuous line, which some believe may
have served as a ceremonial pathway.*

A trapezoid blots out part of a 300-foot bird and a
nearby flower (opposite). Geometric shapes often overprint animal figures
on the Nazca plain, perhaps with some symbolic purpose.

The owl-man (below) overlooks other Nazca figures.
It could bear a message: One arm points skyward, the other to the ground.
Primitive in style, it may predate the animal drawings.

Younger than Nazca's figures, the 500-year-old Fort
Mojave twins may have been warnings to trespassers. More than 200 such
figures dot the California-Arizona desert.

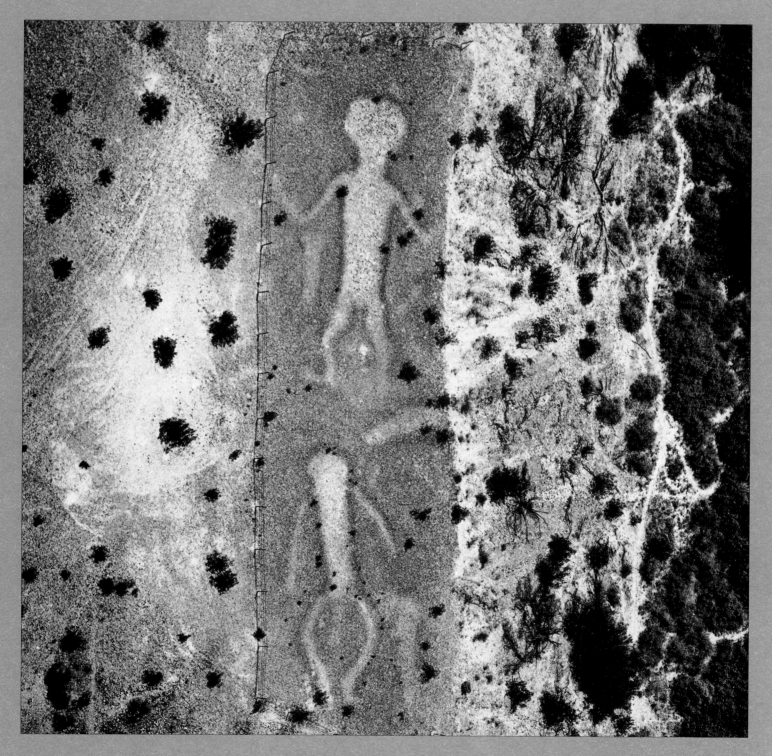

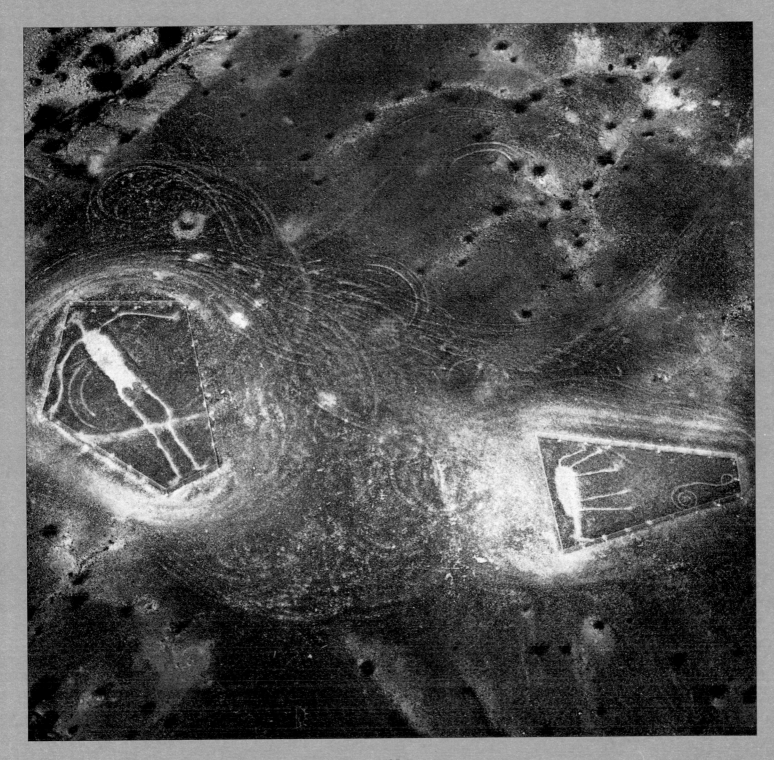

The Blythe Giant and its animal companion yield
scant clues to their origins. Indian legends hint that the figure depicts a
child-eating giant; the animal might be an avenging puma.

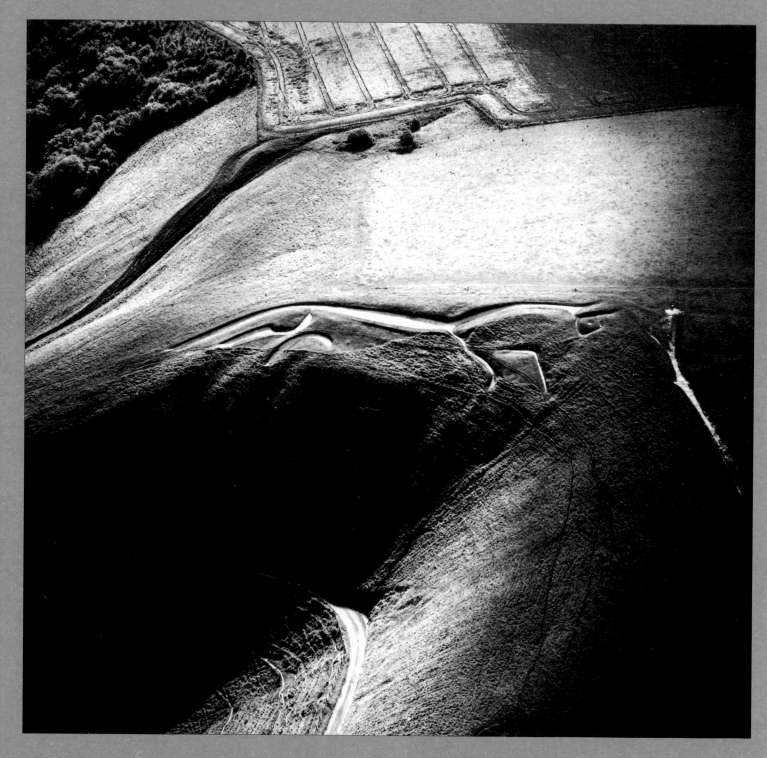

The 365-foot Uffington Horse gallops across a
chalky hillside near Swindon in southwest England. Possibly dating to 100 B.C.,
this effigy is the oldest of more than fifty in Britain.

CHAPTER 5

An Inferior World

O ur ancestors sheltered themselves in caves for many more generations than they have lived in houses. Haunting cave drawings from the dawn of time stand as mute testimony that early humans probed and speculated about the deepest recesses of the earth. Small wonder that the idea of life underground has tugged for so long at the back of the mind.

It has never been an entirely comfortable thought. Cave dwellers sometimes had to wrest their homes from ferocious animals, and the fear that there was yet one more creature in the dark at the back of the cave, or just beyond, must have been widespread. Perhaps that is why the nether world came to be so closely associated with death and dragons, with Satan and the supernatural.

As the human mind developed and took up its endless speculations about the universe, the underground beckoned with as much allure as the stars. While some myths populated the heavens and the remote mountaintops with gods, others saw a hollow earth below, a realm of similarly potent—although frequently less benevolent—deities. When the globe was slowly yielding its secrets to far-flung explorations, travelers who reported finding portals to underground worlds had no less claim to credibility than did those who spoke of new worlds beyond the seas. In time, astonishing claims would be made for a mysterious inner earth peopled with benign giants or Eskimos, evil dwarfs or prehistoric reptiles. Even today, with the world explored, photographed, and plumbed by sophisticated electronic instruments, an element of uncertainty remains. The darkness at the back of the cave has not yet been entirely dispelled.

Hidden worlds beneath the surface of the earth figured prominently in ancient beliefs. Central Asian Buddhists told of the kingdom of Agartha, made up of a worldwide labyrinth of subterranean passages. A haven for the populations of vanished continents, Agartha was a center of intellectual progress and enlightenment. Its holy leader became the King of the World, who, according to one devotee, ''knows all the forces of the world and reads all the souls of humankind and the great book of their destiny.''

The legendary Assyro-Babylonian King Gilgamesh was reported to have had a long conversation about the underworld with the ghost of a dead companion. The Greeks were constantly speculating about the depths of the earth; one myth tells how the musician Orpheus tried in vain to rescue his wife Eurydice from Hades. The poet Homer imagined an underworld waiting to be explored, and the philosopher Plato wrote that there were "tunnels both broad and narrow in the interior" and in the center a god who sits "on the navel of the earth." Egyptians believed in an infernal underground kingdom, and later, Christians had their hell. According to certain tales, the Incas eluded marauding Spanish conquistadors and carried their treasure into deep tunnels that remain secret.

And when science took the place of legend in explaining the world, the underground was not forgotten. One pioneer whose deductions led him below was the brilliant English astronomer Edmond Halley, discoverer of the comet that bears his name. In 1672, while still a schoolboy, Halley became interested in the earth's magnetism.

Halley found that magnetic north was not always in the same place. Studying compass readings taken by himself and others over most of the world, he discerned several patterns of error. For one, local conditions—such as magnetic mineral deposits—might cause a compass needle to deviate. For another, needles were deflected downward, away from horizontal, to a degree that corresponded to latitude. And at various longitudes, compass readings varied laterally from actual magnetic north, in predictable ways that navigators charted and took into account. But the real enigma emerged when Halley examined readings that had been recorded in past times: They showed that variation—the lateral deflection that changed according to longitude—was slowly changing. The only way Halley could explain this phenomenon was to posit the existence of more than one magnetic field. He suggested that the earth is a twin—an outer shell with a separate, inner nucleus. Each of these globes, he proposed, has its own axis, with north and south magnetic poles, and the axes are somewhat inclined to each other. That, along with a slight difference in the velocity of rotation, could cause magnetized needles to seek one or another of the poles—hence the slow shift in the position of magnetic north. Later, when Halley came across readings that could not be accounted for by one interior earth, he added two more, each nestled inside the other like a set of Chinese boxes. "They are," Halley told the Royal Society of London in 1692, "approximately the size of Mars, Venus and Mercury."

Like many other trailblazers of science, Halley felt he had to square his ingenious theory with his religious beliefs. He speculated that since God had stocked every part of the earth's surface with living things, he would have done likewise with the inner world. But this raised another problem, for it seemed self-evident that life requires light. Halley suggested that the interior atmosphere itself is luminous and that the aurora borealis, or northern lights, is caused by the escape of

Battling at the portal to hell, angelic hosts subdue Satan's forces in Pieter Breughel's The Fall

Rebel Angels. Legends usually claim that the hollow earth holds either paradise or perdition.

this glowing essence through the thin crust at the North Pole. During the eighteenth century, as other investigators pushed back the frontiers of knowledge, Halley's ideas were modified but not refuted. The Swiss mathematician Leonhard Euler rejected the idea of multiple planets within, replacing them with a single sun—which he thought provided warmth and light to an advanced inner-earth civiliza-

Seventeenth-century astronomer Edmond Halley holds a diagram of his world theory — a "hypothesis which after Ages may examine, amend or refute."

tion. Later, the Scots mathematician Sir John Leslie determined that there are really two interior suns, which he christened Pluto and Proserpine.

But it would not be a European scientist who first brought international attention to the idea of a world within the earth. That distinction would go instead to a hot-tempered American, a career soldier and man of action from the state of New Jersey.

The son of a judge, John Cleves Symmes was born in 1780 and named for an uncle who had served in the American Revolution. His was hardly the cloistered life of a scholar, although he enjoyed a solid early education and was intensely interested in the natural sciences. In 1802, at the age of twenty-two, he entered the United States Army as an ensign.

From then on, Symmes's life was nomadic and turbulent. In 1807, he insisted on fighting a duel with a fellow officer who had suggested that Symmes was not a gentleman. Both men were shot—Symmes in the wrist and his opponent in the thigh—and suffered from their wounds for the rest of their lives, during which they became good friends. Symmes fought courageously against the British in the War of 1812, once leading his troops in storming a British artillery battery and spiking an enemy cannon with his own hands.

Symmes left the army in 1816 and established a trading post at St. Louis. There, with little else on his hands to do, he indulged in his lifelong passion for reading about the natural sciences. Symmes was especially fascinated by speculation about the formation of the earth, and he began to elaborate with growing enthusiasm and conviction on a theory that may first have occurred to him years before. By the year 1818, Symmes was ready to share his ideas on an international level. He did so in a most spectacular manner. In a letter addressed "To All the World" and sent to politicians, publications, learned societies, and heads of state throughout Europe and America, he wrote: "I declare the earth is hollow, and habitable within; containing a number of solid concentrick spheres, one within the other, and that it is open at the poles 12 or 16 degrees; I pledge my life," he continued, "in support of this truth, and am ready to explore the hollow, if the world will support and aid me in the undertaking."

Symmes assured his readers that he would prove his case in greater detail with a subsequent publication. For skeptics, he included a character reference and a testimonial to his sanity signed by local physicians and businessmen. Then Symmes asked for "one hundred brave companions, well equipped, to start from Siberia in the fall season, with Reindeer and sleighs, on the ice of the frozen sea; I engage we find warm and rich land, stocked with thrifty vegetables and animals if not men, on reaching one degree northward of latitude 82; we will return in the succeeding spring."

But instead of the support and aid Symmes had requested, the public responded with hoots of derisive laughter. He, his theory, and his audacity were ridiculed in newspapers and scientific journals the world over.

Undeterred, Symmes launched a vigorous campaign of

newspaper articles, more open letters, and countless lectures around the country. Over and over he argued that a mass of spinning, unformed matter—such as the earth once was—could not have organized itself into a solid sphere. Centrifugal force throws rotating matter away from the axis of rotation; gravity pulls it inward. When the forces balance, he said, the result is a belt of material with the densest matter outermost and the axis open. In this way, Symmes claimed, the materials of the earth were organized as concentric, hollow spheres open at the poles.

Symmes marshaled all kinds of evidence, from the astronomical to the commonplace, to support his scheme. Look at the concentric rings of Saturn, the polar caps of Mars, he said; look at how a cup of sand, rotated, will sort itself into concentric circles according to its density. He appealed to religion: Nature, he pointed out, was a great economist of matter, having opted wherever feasible for hollow construction—hollow bones, stalks, quills, and hairs. Furthermore, he said, God would not have created a vast inner world only to leave it barren and empty. Somehow Symmes reasoned from the general to the particular and developed specific dimensions for the multiple earths he envisioned. The known world, the outermost of five, he said, has an open-

ing 4,000 miles across at the North Pole and another, 6,000 miles in diameter, at the South. One could walk into these openings, for they are inclined into the earth's thousand-mile-thick crust at a gentle angle. Anyone who did so would find within a gentle, sheltered land warmed by the indirect rays of the sun shining in at the polar portholes.

Symmes spoke relentlessly to all who would listen to him, pouring out great, disorganized jumbles of his thought. His fervent speeches drew large crowds of the curious but, for the most part, elicited only amusement or mild interest instead of cash for his arctic expedition. He did make a few converts, however—among whom the most significant were an Ohio newspaper editor named Jeremiah N. Reynolds, who began giving his own lectures in support of Symmes's theories, and a wealthy Ohioan named James McBride.

It may well have been McBride who requested Kentucky Senator Richard M. Johnson—who later served as vice president in the administration of Martin Van Buren—to introduce in Congress a petition for funding the proposed expedition. It was tabled. McBride then compiled a book summarizing, in a more concise and logical fashion than Symmes ever did, the theory of concentric spheres (which was more popularly and

John Cleves Symmes's handmade wooden globe dramatizes his contention that the earth's interior is accessible through vast openings at the poles.

rudely referred to as the Theory of Symmes's Hole). But it was all for nothing. The strain of ten years of vigorous proselytizing broke Symmes's health, and he died in 1829 without seeing his theory accepted or his expedition mounted.

Symmes had clearly hoped that his quest would bring him monumental renown. Indeed, using the pen name of Captain Adam Seaborn, he published in 1820 a fictional account of a voyage to the earth's interior, entitled *Symzonia; Voyage of Discovery,* in which he spelled out the class of glory he hoped would be his. As Captain Seaborn prepares to land at a subterranean utopia peopled with gentle, fair-skinned beings, he muses: "I was about to secure to my name a conspicuous and imperishable place on the tablets of History, and a niche of the first order in the temple of Fame. . . . The voyage of Columbus was but an excursion on a fish pond, and his discoveries, compared with mine, were but trifles."

That, of course, was not the way the world saw it, and after his death Symmes's vision of a hollow earth was nearly forgotten. The polar expedition he had so long espoused, however, was another matter

In fact, Congress authorized such a voyage in 1828, the year before Symmes died. This was in part the result of vigorous lobbying by Jeremiah Reynolds, who instead of appealing to scientific curiosity stressed the trade to be opened and territory to be claimed. The idea gained the support of President John Quincy Adams but not of Andrew Jackson, who succeeded Adams as president in 1829. The expedition would not sail for another decade.

Meanwhile, the impatient Reynolds joined a sealing and exploring expedition to the South Seas aboard the *Annawan.* (A magazine story that he wrote on his return—*Mocha Dick, or, The White Whale of the Pacific*—may have been an inspiration for Herman Melville's masterpiece *Moby Dick,* published twelve years later.) On his return, Reynolds renewed earlier calls to sealers and whalers to add their voices to the clamor for an expedition, now proposed for Antarctica.

In an 1836 speech given in the U.S. Capitol's Hall of Representatives, Reynolds conjured a stirring vision of American ships casting anchor at the South Pole—"that point where all the meridians terminate, where our eagle and star-spangled banner may be unfurled and planted, and left to wave on the axis of the earth itself!" If he still believed in Symmes's Hole at that point, Reynolds kept it to himself.

Swayed by such patriotic fervor, and by the appeals of the whalers and other commercial interests, Congress finally approved the expedition and provided $300,000 for it. However, two years dragged by before it actually departed. By that time, the impassioned Reynolds had so roundly denounced the Secretary of the Navy for dawdling that Reynolds's name

was ultimately struck from the expedition roster when the ships finally sailed in 1838.

Named for its commander, Navy Lieutenant Charles Wilkes, the four-year Wilkes expedition—the first to team civilian scientists with naval crews—did indeed make important discoveries, but not those that Symmes had so fondly hoped for. Instead of charting a polar opening, the voyagers returned with maps of thousands of miles of antarctic coastline, having proved that this little-known landmass is in fact big enough to qualify as the earth's seventh continent.

Like Symmes before him, Reynolds found that the tangible rewards for his devotion were slim. An expedition botanist who discovered a new genus of ivy in Samoa on the southward journey named it *Reynoldsia* in honor of Reynolds's "unflagging zeal." And Reynolds apparently wielded considerable influence over the fevered mind of one of America's greatest authors, Edgar Allan Poe. In the short story "MS Found in a Bottle" and his novel *The Narrative of Arthur Gordon Pym of Nantucket,* Poe describes doomed voyages that end with ships being sucked into a watery abyss at the South

Pole—ideas founded on the hollow-earth writings of Reynolds. Although the two probably never met, Poe was calling Reynolds's name when he died in a Baltimore hospital in 1849.

Such stimulation of fiction writers by scientific speculations was a hallmark of the nineteenth century, and many novelistic excursions were so plausibly presented that readers were sometimes hard pressed to separate the real from the imaginary. Nowhere did flights of literary fancy seem so credible—or foretell the future more accurately—than in the writings of Jules Verne. With remarkable prescience, he envisioned submarines prowling the ocean depths, aeronauts circumnavigating the globe, and astronauts traveling to the moon. One of his first ventures into his special world, where fact and fantasy were nearly indistinguishable, was his *Journey to the Centre of the Earth.*

The story begins in 1863 in Hamburg, Germany, where Otto Lidenbrock, an eccentric professor of mineralogy, has deciphered a coded, runic document from Iceland. It turns out to be directions for reaching the center of the earth. Lidenbrock and his nephew Axel immediately go to Iceland, hire a guide, and descend the chimney of an extinct volcano into the depths of the earth. They make their way through hazardous passages and survive the tortures of thirst to discover, eighty-eight miles down, a vast sea. What amazes them the most, after their long ordeal in a series of labyrinthine tunnels, is the brightness of the underground world. Declares Axel: "It was like an aurora borealis, a continuous cosmic phenomenon, filling a cavern big enough to contain an ocean."

They construct a raft and sail across this mysterious ocean, discovering a lost world of giant plants and prehistoric reptiles. Throughout, the professor remains the model of a rational nineteenth-century scientist. He speculates that the ocean had flowed down from the surface through a fissure, now closed, and that some of the water had evaporated to cause clouds and storms. Reflects the nephew: "This theory about the phenomena we had witnessed struck me as satisfactory, for however great the wonders of Nature may be, they can always be explained by physical laws." Eventually, they are lofted by a volcanic eruption to the island of Stromboli, off the coast of Italy—having traveled under the whole of Europe—and return to a hero's welcome in Hamburg. As a touch of verisimilitude, Verne's story includes a reference to Sir John Leslie, the eighteenth-century mathematician who proposed the theory of a hollow earth that is lit by twin suns, Pluto and Proserpina. And at one point, young Axel wonders aloud about Leslie's theory: "Could he have been telling the truth?"

The same question was often asked of *The Coming Race,* a novel by Lord Lytton, published following his death in 1873. Edward Bulwer-Lytton, as this English peer was first known, was the author of a celebrated historical novel, *The Last Days of Pompeii,* and a member of several mystical societies. His story, like Jules Verne's, begins with the chance discovery of an opening into an underground world. But what Lytton's narrator finds there is far more ominous than Verne's imaginings.

He enters a mine shaft, penetrates a fissure on a lamp-lit road, and finds himself amid a race of supermen. He learns that in the world of the Vril-ya, as these handsome giants call themselves, all human dreams have been realized. War and social conflict have been abolished. Machines perform the menial chores; people are free to do what they prefer and a storekeeper is as highly regarded as the chief magistrate. Crime, drunkenness, and other vices are unknown, and everyone lives past a hundred years of age in vigorous health.

*Explorers follow a tunnel
underground in this engraving from
Journey to the Centre of the Earth.*

All of these blessings derive from "vril," a versatile fluid that gives these people absolute mastery over all forms of matter. It allows them to fly on artificial wings, to heal and preserve, to light their cities, and to blast away rocks for the creation of new settlements. Its destructive power is so awesome that war has been outlawed.

In this interior world is an ideal society that lives its motto: "No happiness without order, no order without authority, no authority without unity." But Lytton's narrator soon realizes that all is not well. "If you were to take a thousand of the best and most philosophical human beings you could find," he muses, "and place them as citizens in this beautified community, I believe that in less than a year they would either die of boredom or attempt some revolution." He begins dreaming of a glass of whisky and a juicy steak, with a cigar to follow.

The Vril-ya realize that this imperfect earthling is a disruptive force. But he must not be allowed to leave; the Vril-ya intend to return to the upper world, where they originated, and supplant the inferior races that now live there. They resolve to kill Lytton's narrator, but he is rescued by the Vril-ya woman who loves him, and he ascends into the mine shaft supported on her wings.

He ends his account with a chilling message: "Being frankly told by my physician that I am afflicted by a complaint which, though it gives little pain and no perceptible notice of its encroachments, may at any moment be fatal, I have thought it my duty to my fellow-men to place on record these forewarnings of THE COMING RACE."

At about the same time that Lytton was writing his curious book—which would later become entrenched as a part of occultist lore—an American herbalist was upending the whole idea of a hollow earth. This mysterious realm is not to be found below us, proposed Cyrus Read Teed, but above us; we are not on the globe, but in it.

Born on a New York farm in 1839, Teed served as a corporal in the Union Army during the Civil War before setting up his practice of herbal cures. He read widely and found that the scientifically accepted theories of an infinite universe were a threat and an affront to his devout sensibilities. Teed dreamed instead of a more compact and comprehensible cosmos. When he finally conceived of his own theory, he considered it to be not only a scientific revelation but a religious one as well.

Teed expounded on his notions in a book entitled *The Cellular Cosmogony, or, the Earth a Concave Sphere,* which he wrote under the pseudonym of Koresh, the Hebrew name for Cyrus. The known world is on the concave, inner surface of a sphere, he explained, outside of which there is only a void. At the center of the sphere, the rotating sun, half dark and half light, gives an illusion of rising and setting. The moon is a reflection of the earth's surface; the stars and planets reflect from metallic planes on the earth's concave surface. The vast internal cavity is filled with a dense atmosphere that makes it impossible to see across the globe to the lands and peoples on other sides.

Odd as this vision was, it turned out that it could not be disproved mathematically. Indeed, Teed—who took Koresh as his permanent name—offered a $10,000 reward to anyone who could confute his theory, but he found no takers. When a scientist would use geometric inversion to turn a sphere inside out and map external points in their corresponding internal position, the result would be a universe that looks like the one described by Teed, or Koresh. But Teed did not need the validation of mathematics: "To know of the earth's concavity," he wrote, "is to know God, while to believe in the earth's convexity is to deny Him and all His works."

Captivated by his vision, Teed abandoned medicine and proclaimed himself the messiah of a new religion called Koreshanity. To help spread his gospel, he formed a church, established the World's College of Life in Chicago, and began publishing *The Flaming Sword*—a magazine that continued to appear until 1949. With the disciples and donations attracted by his impassioned lectures—and spurred by threats from irate husbands whose wives had abandoned them to join the Koreshans—he bought a 300-acre tract near Fort Meyers, Florida, in 1894 and founded a community he called the Koreshan Unity, Inc. It was meant to be a home for 10 million converts but only 250 actually settled there. They were fiercely loyal, however, and when Teed died in 1908, his followers mounted a vigil, waiting for him to rise again and carry them with him to heaven, as he had prophesied. The hoped-for ascension did not come to pass; after four days, the local health officer ordered a conventional burial.

True to form, Teed's interment was anything but conventional. He was laid to rest in an immense mausoleum with a twenty-four-hour guard—until his tomb was washed away by a hurricane in 1921. Forty years later, his tract was turned into the Koreshan State Historic Site, and Koresh's disciples offered guided tours until the last one died in 1982.

As the twentieth century began, it might have seemed that the idea of a hollow earth would become more and more difficult to sustain. Explorers, after all, were combing the world's surface at an ever-faster clip. But the new information that they brought back did not put an end to hollow-earth speculations. Indeed, two new proponents—William Reed and Marshall B. Gardner—weighed in with major contributions to the field.

The two theorists were stimulated by some anomalous discoveries by polar explorers. For one thing, according to many accounts, water and air temperatures grew warmer with proximity to the North Pole. Fridtjof Nansen, the Norwegian explorer and statesman, reported from far inside the Arctic Circle that it was almost too warm to sleep. He observed that winds from the north seemed to raise the temperature, whereas south winds lowered it.

Other travelers reported similar warming trends and described seeing abundant wildlife—birds, mammals, and plagues of mosquitoes—encountered at high latitudes. Many of these creatures appeared to be migrating north, rather than south, and were seen to be returning from sojourns in what should have been barren regions looking sleek and well fed. There were accounts, too, of travelers who saw multicolored snow—red, green, yellow, and black.

An even more arresting mystery had been created in 1846 by the discovery of a long-extinct woolly mammoth frozen in the ice of Siberia. So well had the creature been preserved in the arctic cold that its stomach still contained identifiable traces of its last meal of pine cones and fir branches. Scientists wondered how the enormous animal could have been frozen quickly enough to arrest its digestive processes—which normally would continue even after death. Some theorized that the mammoth had lived near the pole when the climate was much warmer and had succumbed to a sudden freeze. Marshall Gardner, among others, claimed no climate change could have been that sudden.

In his book *A Journey to the Earth's Interior, or, Have the Poles Really Been Discovered,* published in 1913, Gardner devoted a full chapter to the mammoth mystery. The explanation, he said, was simple: Mammoths had not become extinct at all but are "wandering today in the interior of the earth. When he ventures too near the polar orifice . . . , he becomes stranded on a breaking ice floe and carried over from the interior regions, to the outer regions or perhaps falls in a crevasse in ice, which afterwards begins to move in some great glacial movement. In these ways the bodies are carried over to Siberia and left where we have seen them discovered."

Reed, in his book *The Phantom of the Poles,* had an explanation for the colored snow reported by travelers. The red, green, and yellow must be pollen, he said; the black would be soot from volcanoes. And all must have come from the earth's interior, the closest possible source. Accounting for the polar

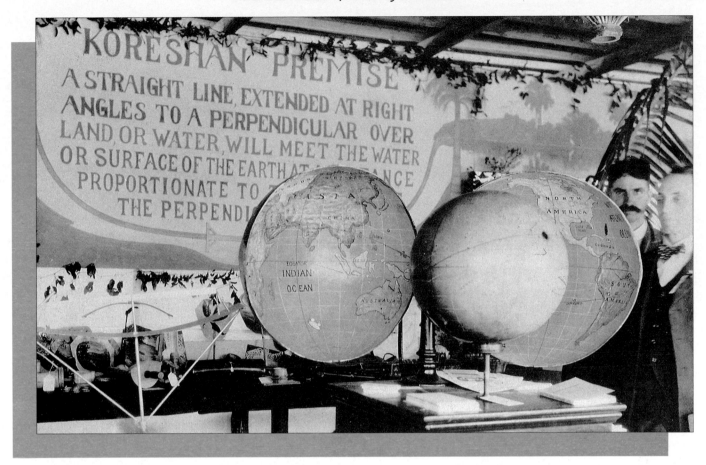

warming was more complex, but Gardner and Reed both attributed it to Symmes-like openings into the inner earth. Reed described the earth's crust as 800 miles thick, with gravity acting toward the deepest part of the shell. In other words, the same gravity that pulled objects on the outside of the sphere inward would thrust objects inside the globe outward. Voyagers could thus sail over the edge of the polar openings without being aware that they had left one world for another. Indeed, Reed insisted that "all, or nearly all, of the explorers have spent much of their time past the turning-point, and have had a look at the interior of the earth."

Gardner believed that the interior was lit by a central sun, possibly 600 miles in diameter, left over from the spinning nebula from which the earth was formed. Mars had been formed in similar fashion, he wrote, and its interior sun could sometimes be seen glinting through its polar openings. Reflected light from the earth's interior sun, according to Gardner, creates the startling brilliance of the aurora borealis at the North Pole and the aurora australis at the South Pole.

On this subject, Gardner parted company with Reed, who maintained that the inner world got its light from the outer sun shining in at the poles. As for the auroras, Reed had an ingenious explanation. The northern lights, he said, are the reflected images of interior prairie fires or volcanoes. They obviously are not caused by electricity, as orthodox scientists had proposed. This theory Reed disposed of with a scornful, rhetorical question: "Does electricity ever move through the heavens as if driven slowly along by some unseen agency?" To explain why the aurora is most brilliant during the arctic winter, Reed pointed out that the sun shines directly into the south polar opening at that time of year. The ice and snow at the rim reflect and intensify the light that emerges from the North Pole to create the aurora. Presumably, the situation is reversed in summer.

Reed was eager to see the inner earth, with its "vast continents, oceans, mountains and rivers, vegetable and animal life," put to use. And by his reckoning, the interior "can be made accessible to mankind with one-fourth the outlay of treasure, time, and life that it cost to build the subway in New York City. The number of people that can find comfortable homes (if it be not already occupied) will be billions."

For his part, Gardner thought that at least some of the interior was already peopled by Eskimos, who must have originated there. As evidence, he cited Eskimo myths about a warm homeland to the north of the arctic. He reasoned that the Eskimos must have migrated to the ice-bound region where they now live because it was easier to hunt whales and seals there than it was in open water.

What really fired Gardner's imagination was the prospect of mining the interior, where he expected to find bountiful lodes of gold, platinum, and diamonds. "Our country has the men, the aeroplanes, the enterprise, and the capital," he declared, to appropriate these treasures. But he was not suggesting that the exploration be done out of greed; rather, it was the duty of America, Gardner believed, "with her high civilization, her free institutions, her humanity—for there may be native population to deal with—her generosity," to move quickly. "Do we want one of the autocratic countries of Europe to perpetuate in this new world all the old evils of colonial oppression and exploitation?" he asked.

While Reed and Gardner were content to theorize about the inner earth, Olaf Jansen claimed actually to have been there. Jansen was a Norwegian sailor who retired to Glendale, California, in the early 1900s. Just before he died, at the age of ninety-five, he told writer Willis George Emerson, one of his few friends, an incredible story, which Emerson published in 1908 under the title *The Smoky God, or, a Voyage to the Inner World*. Jansen had waited to reveal the truth, he explained, because when he first tried to tell his story, he was locked in an asylum for twenty-eight years.

As a teen-age boy in 1829, Jansen related, he sailed with his father to Franz Joseph Land, a group of islands high above the Arctic Circle, in search of ivory tusks. Finding open seas and fair weather, they resolved to explore unknown waters to the north. A storm drove them through a barrier of fog and snow, nearly capsizing their frail sloop, and delivered them to a cloudless calm beyond. They sailed on in fine weather and spied a smoky, furnace-colored sun, which turned out to be a so-called Smoky God that was worshipped as a deity by the inhabitants of the inner world they had entered.

There the Jansens met with a race of good-humored giants, ten to twelve feet tall. They visited a seaport city that was surrounded by vineyards and richly ornamented with gold; they saw a forest of trees that would make the California redwoods seem like underbrush, and they ate grapes as large as oranges. They were whisked by monorail to the city of Eden, where they met the great high priest in a palace paved with gold and jewels.

After two and a half years in this paradise, the homesick father and son were allowed to leave. Carrying bags of gold nuggets, they sailed through the south polar opening. The elder Jansen was drowned when an iceberg crushed their sloop, but Olaf was rescued by a Scottish whaler.

In support of his fantastic tale, Jansen called on some of the same evidence that Reed and Gardner had used in their theorizing. He mentioned magnetic irregularities at the poles, wind-blown pollen, and mammoth bones in Siberia. And he believed that a party of Swedish polar explorers, lost in a balloon after leaving Spitsbergen in 1897, "are now in the 'within' world, and doubtless are being entertained, as my father and myself were entertained, by the kindhearted giant race inhabiting the inner Atlantic Continent."

All of these inner-earth visionaries suffered for their beliefs. Jansen was locked up; Reed and Gardner were ridiculed. But Gardner, for one, was equally intolerant of fellow enthusiasts. He dismissed Symmes's theory as merely "supposition" and declared: "Of course it is very easy for anyone to deny all the facts of science and get up some purely private explanation of the formation of the earth. The man who does that is a crank. Unfortunately the man in the street does not always discriminate between a crank and a scientist."

Gardner was enraged to discover that some scientists had the same difficulty and relegated his own work to the crank category. For example, the director of the Lick Observatory of Santa Cruz, California, wrote to him: "It may be a disappointment to you to learn that we are placing your book in the class which contains pamphlets which we perennially receive on such subjects as 'The Earth is Flat,' etc. It is surprising how many of these contributions there are which ignore, with apparent deliberation, the great body of modern scientific knowledge."

"Sheer misrepresentation," fulminated Gardner, who preferred to quote more favorable opinions from a Professor A. Schmidt of Stuttgart ("a very weighty physical hypothesis") and Professor H. Sjogren of Stockholm ("originality and audacity"). Gardner remained unshaken in his beliefs despite the increasing number of explorers—such as Cook, Peary, Scott, and Amundsen—who said they had been to the poles and had observed no openings into the earth. These naysayers were, said Gardner, mistaken. The future would prove him correct: "We shall see all when we explore the Arctic in earnest, as we shall easily be able to do with the aid of airships."

Before full-scale aerial surveys of the poles could shed much light on the polar regions, a kind of dark age intervened, during which exploration and scientific progress were overshadowed by war and tyranny. In 1933, Adolf Hitler proclaimed himself the leader of a Thousand Year Reich, a civilization of supermen that would rule the world. The Nazi philosophy was based on a belief in the supremacy of the Aryan race, and strenuous efforts were made to buttress this claim with evidence dredged from history, folklore, and science. In this atmosphere of myth, hollow-earth theories thrived.

Peter Bender, a German aviator who was seriously wounded in World War I, attracted favorable attention in Germany during the 1930s with his elaborations on Koreshanity. Top Nazi leaders, including Hitler, reportedly took seriously the concept of a concave world that was first proposed by Cyrus "Koresh" Teed. And it appears that these leaders sometimes translated their beliefs into concrete actions.

In April 1942, for example, at the height of the war, Dr. Heinz Fischer, an expert on infrared radiation, purportedly led a group of technicians on a secret expedition to the Baltic island of Rügen. The men aimed a powerful camera loaded with infrared film into the sky at a forty-five-degree angle and left it in this position for several days. The goal, which proved elusive, was to take a picture of the British fleet across the hollow interior of the concave earth.

Other beliefs about inner worlds gained currency among Nazi enthusiasts. There was, for example, a Vril Society, also known as the Luminous Lodge, which held that Lord Lytton's book *The Coming Race* was true and that it offered a blueprint for the future. Members of this occultist body no doubt thrilled to the Vril-ya slogan—"No happiness without order, no order without authority, no authority without unity." But developing a race of supermen was difficult and took time. The Luminous Lodge wanted to make contact with any existing race of superior beings, in the hope of establishing peaceful relations and learning their secrets.

Other organizations followed similar urges. The anti-Semitic Thule Society of Bavaria, whose adherents included Nazi philosopher Alfred Rosenberg and deputy führer Rudolf Hess, sometimes claimed to represent survivors of Atlantis who lived in the Himalayas—the legendary secret chiefs of Tibet. Some of the society's more enthusiastic members believed that they could contact their master, the King of Fear, by use of tarot cards.

According to some accounts, Hitler may even have believed that he had seen a member of a superrace from the inner earth. He reportedly told Hermann Rauschning, the Nazi governor of Danzig: "The new man is living amongst us now! He is here! . . . I will tell you a secret. I have seen the new man. He is intrepid and cruel. I was afraid of him." The führer was also rumored to have dispatched expeditions to Tibet and Mongolia in search of underground wisdom. In further pursuit of such knowledge, special units are said to have scoured the mines and caverns of occupied Europe for passages leading to a subterranean world. And then there is the recurring legend that senior Nazis took refuge in the bowels of the earth as Germany collapsed in ruins.

By then, the airborne explorations of the poles envisioned by Gardner were well under way. In 1926, United States Navy aviator Richard E. Byrd had become the first to fly over the North Pole; three years later, he made the first flight over the South Pole. He would cross the South Pole by air twice more, in 1947 and 1955.

His findings were hardly calculated to bring cheer to diehard hollow-earthers. Byrd reported that he flew an enormous triangle around the South Pole, "surveyed nearly 10,000 square miles of the country beyond the Pole," and found nothing. "Although it is somewhat disappointing to report," he wrote, "there was no observable feature of any significance beyond the Pole. There was only the rolling white desert from horizon to horizon."

Elsewhere on the continent, the landscape appeared more varied. Byrd found jagged mountains of coal black and brick red, where ice-covered rocks reflected the sun "in an indescribable complex of colors, blends of blues, purples, and greens such as man seldom has seen before." Greatly impressed by this natural beauty, Byrd became almost lyrical: "At the bottom of this planet lies an enchanted continent in the sky. Sinister and beautiful she lies in her frozen slumber, her billowy white robes of snow weirdly luminous with amethysts and emeralds of ice."

Byrd's discoveries did little to end speculations about a hollow earth, open at the poles; on the contrary, believers were stimulated to new heights of endeavor—and confusion over dates and places—to discredit Byrd's reports. In 1959, two years after the polar explorer's death, a writer named F. Amadeo Giannini insisted, in a book entitled *Worlds beyond the Poles*, that Byrd had in fact flown into the inner earth—1,700 miles beyond the North Pole in 1947 and 2,300 miles beyond the South Pole in 1956.

Others, including pulp magazine editor Ray Palmer and the highly imaginative author Raymond Bernard, shared a be-

---

Adolf Hitler is rumored to have dispatched several expeditions to search for proof of a hollow earth.

lief that someone was conspiring to keep Byrd's real findings secret. They found confirming evidence in Byrd's phrases about "the country beyond" and "the enchanted continent in the sky." And they claimed to have discovered other radio messages that told of iceless land and lakes, mountains covered with trees, and even a monstrous animal resembling the mammoth of antiquity moving through allegedly polar underbrush.

Palmer, for one, had a considerable professional interest in keeping alive the notion of habitable regions beneath the earth. As editor of the magazine *Amazing Stories,* he started publishing in the mid-1940s a long-running series of articles by Richard S. Shaver, a Pennsylvania welder who claimed to have stumbled upon a race of underground creatures called deros. According to Shaver's sensational account, the deros were survivors of the lost land of Lemuria and used mysterious rays to influence events on the earth's surface.

As Shaver had it, deros were to blame for all the evils that plague humankind. Every mishap, from airplane crashes to sprained ankles, could be traced to machinations of the deros. Once, after Shaver had visited with Palmer, the editor experienced an amazing infestation of fleas. Queried about the sudden appearance of the vermin, Shaver insisted that he had never been troubled with fleas. Surely, he said, it was the work of the deros.

Palmer cheerfully billed the Shaver tales as "something NEW in science fiction." But as sales of his magazine soared on the strength of disclosures about the deros, he was deluged with earnest letters from readers who reported that they, too, had encountered the subterranean beings. Some told of harrowing adventures. One correspondent warned that Palmer was "playing with dynamite" in exposing the deros. He and a companion, he wrote, had once fought their way out of a cave with submachine guns, and still bore the scars of wounds inflicted by vicious creatures. "Don't print our names," he pleaded. "We are not cowards, but we are not crazy." Contemplating Shaver's revelation—which would forever after be known in occultist circles as the Shaver Mystery—Palmer could only conclude: "If it is a delusion, many people have it."

Others also shared with Palmer and Bernard the belief that there was more to the Byrd story than had been revealed. A woman wrote to Palmer claiming that, in 1929 in White Plains, New York, she had been able to see a newsreel of Byrd's 1926 flight over the North Pole, in which Byrd "exclaimed in wonder as he approached a warm-water lake surrounded by conifers, with a large animal moving about among the trees." No such newsreel was ever found, and the reported radio broadcasts found no place in Byrd's detailed accounts of his antarctic expedition. Bernard suggested darkly that they may have been suppressed by secret forces. The truth of Admiral Byrd's discoveries, he declared, remains "a leading international top secret."

But the diehards soon had more difficult evidence to deal with. In March of 1959, the U.S. nuclear submarine *Skate,* having sailed under the arctic ice pack, surfaced at the North Pole. The crew used inertial navigation equipment to calculate the speed of the earth's rotation and thus to confirm arrival at the pole, where the rotation settles to a single point. The skipper, Commander James F. Calvert, wrote later: "We took exhaustively careful soundings, gravity measurements, and navigation readings to ensure that we had attained the precise navigational Pole, and had as much data as possible from the famous spot."

Palmer had little to say about the *Skate* expedition, but he returned triumphantly to the fray in 1970. "THE HOLE! . . . NOW WE HAVE A PHOTO!" he proclaimed in *Flying Saucers* magazine, which he had launched in 1957. And indeed he did have a picture, courtesy of the Environmental Science Service Administration of the U.S. Department of Commerce. It was one of a series of about 40,000 satellite photos of the earth and showed what looked to be a gaping, circular black spot or void around the North Pole. "How many more photos will we require to establish a fact?" demanded Palmer, claiming that the supposed opening was concealed by clouds on all the other satellite photographs.

Sadly for Palmer the photograph turned out to be not quite what it appeared. In fact it was not a conventional photo

Richard Byrd uses a nonmagnetic sun compass to find his position over Antarctica. Byrd's reports from the pole convinced some hollow-earth enthusiasts that he had located a hidden world.

computer-generated image of the earth's interior. It has long been generally agreed that the earth has three principal layers: a solid crust of granite and basalt that averages twenty-five miles in thickness; a 2,000-mile-thick mantle of viscous rock; and a central core of molten iron and nickel, 4,000 miles in diameter. Scientists have assumed that the inner core is a smooth sphere, but images examined in the mid-1980s show instead a lumpy blob, with mountains several miles high and canyons six times deeper than the Grand Canyon. Researchers speculate that the mountains were caused by ponderous currents in the molten mantle, where hotter, less dense areas rise from the core like hot air from a radiator; cooler regions closer to the crust sink toward the core. Such movements could well push up some areas of the core and depress others. But the belief in the world within the earth is far too durable to yield even to reams of computer printouts or acres of satellite images. There are always contradictions in the data or obscure areas in the images, always room for a dedicated believer to wedge in doubt and cling to a contrary notion.

at all, but a mosaic of television images transmitted by an orbiting satellite. The images, taken during a twenty-four-hour period from many points along the satellite's orbit, were processed by a computer and reassembled to form a composite view of Earth as if seen from a single point directly over the North Pole. During this time, regions near the Pole were shrouded by the continuous darkness of the northern winter. Hence an unlighted area occupies the center of the picture.

But the hardy believers in the existence of a world within persist despite daunting accumulations of evidence to the contrary. They point out that no one has penetrated very far beneath the earth's crust, and they take heart from the fact that despite technological advances, modern scientists hold different theories about what is to be found there.

Indeed, earth scientists continue to encounter the unexpected. Soundings of the planet's depths, taken with instruments that analyze shock waves from earthquakes and man-made explosions, have turned up considerable surprises. The technique, called seismic tomography, uses the analyses of thousands of earthquakes over a multiyear period to create a

Thus the dark at the back of the cave persists, along with a deep-seated need to know for sure what is there—not by abstract calculation or inference, but for certain. Beyond that, there is the compulsion to envision better worlds, where intractable human problems have been solved, where the future is under benevolent control. There is an almost instinctive human eagerness to follow the path of any dim trail of anomalous clues when there is a possibility that it will lead to a shining or secret place, whether it be Agartha under the earth, Atlantis beneath the sea, or a ring of stones pulsing with primeval energies. Proving that such places or things do not exist is not enough. It is hardly relevant. The mysteries will remain as long as there are those to ponder them.

ACKNOWLEDGMENTS

The index was prepared by Lynne R. Hobbs. The editors wish to thank the following individuals and institutions for their valuable assistance in the preparation of this volume:

American Society of Dowsers, Danville, Vt.; Association for Research and Enlightenment, Virginia Beach; Jo Bigelow, president, The Koreshan Unity, Inc., Estero, Fla.; Christopher Bird, Molokai, Hawaii; John Bromley, Ethos Consultants Ltd., Medicine Hat, Alberta, Canada; Cahokia Mounds Museum, Collinsville, Ill.; Stuart W. Conner, Billings, Mont.; Bill Cox, editor, *Life Understanding Newsletter,* Santa Barbara, Calif.; Paul Devereux, Brecon, Powys, Wales; Dianne Dubler, New York; Hilary Evans, London; Bruce Gernon, Jr., Islamorada, Fla.; Bob Girard, Scotia, N.Y.; Dr. Gerald Hawkins, Washington, D.C.; Historic New Orleans Collection, New Orleans; Robert Humphris, Department of Mechanical Engineering, University of Virginia, Charlottesville; Lt. Col. A. S. Jenkins, T.D., Wisbech, Cambridgeshire, England; Mark Lehner, New Haven, Conn.; Ian Lowe, The Ashmolean Museum, Oxford, England; John Michell, London; Minnesota Historical Society, St. Paul; National Spiritual Science Center, Washington, D.C.; Naval Aviation History, Washington, D.C.; Toyne Newton, Worthing, Sussex, England; Peruvian Embassy, Washington, D.C.; Roslyn Strong, North Edgecomb, Maine; Charles Walker, Worthing, Sussex, England; Jim Woodman, Miami, Fla.

BIBLIOGRAPHY

Atkinson, R.J.C., *Stonehenge.* Harmondsworth, Middlesex, England: Penguin Books Ltd., 1979.

Aveni, Anthony F.:
Archaeoastronomy in Pre-Columbian America. Austin: University of Texas Press, 1975.
"The Nazca Lines: Patterns in the Desert." *Archaeology,* July/August 1986.

Cavendish, Richard, ed., *Man, Myth & Magic: The Illustrated Encyclopedia of Mythology, Religion and the Unknown.* New York: Marshall Cavendish, 1985.

Cayce, Edgar Evans, *Edgar Cayce on Atlantis.* New York: Paperback Inc., 1962.

Cazeau, Charles J., and Stuart D. Scott, Jr., *Exploring the Unknown: Great Mysteries Reexamined.* New York: Plenum Press, 1979.

Chippendale, Christopher, *Stonehenge Complete.* Ithaca, N.Y.: Cornell University Press, 1983.

Churchward, James, *The Lost Continent of Mu.* New York: I. Washburn, 1931.

Crookson, Peter, ed., *The Ages of Man.* New York: St. Martin's Press, 1983.

Cyr, Donald L., ed., *Stonehenge Viewpoint,* nos. 23-29. Santa Barbara, 1985.

Dalton, John N., comp., *The Cruise of Her Majesty's Ship "Bacchante" 1879-1882.* London: Macmillan, 1886.

De Camp, L. Sprague, *Lost Continents: The Atlantis Theme in History, Science and Literature.* New York: Dover, 1970.

Devereux, Paul, *Earth Lights: Towards an Explanation of the UFO Enigma.* Wellingborough, Northampton, England: Turnstone Press Ltd., 1982.

Devereux, Paul, and Ian Thomson, *The Leyhunters Companion.* London: Thames and Hudson Ltd., 1979.

Donnelly, Ignatius, *Atlantis: The Antediluvian World.* New York: Gramercy, 1985.

Edgerton, Harold E., "Stonehenge—New Light on an Old Riddle," *National Geographic,* June 1960.

Edward, I.E.S., *The Pyramids of Egypt.* Harmondsworth, Middlesex, England: Penguin, 1985.

Evans, Humphrey, *The Mystery of the Pyramids.* New York: Thomas Y. Crowell, 1979.

Fawcett, P. H., *Exploration Fawcett.* London: Hutchinson, 1953.

Fay, Charles Eday, *Mary Celeste: The Odyssey of an Abandoned Ship.* Salem, Mass.: Peabody Museum of Salem, 1942.

Ferris, Timothy, "Playboy Interview: Erich von Däniken." *Playboy,* August 1974.

Fix, William R., *Pyramid Odyssey.* Urbanna, Va.: Mercury Media, 1984.

Gardner, Marshall B., *A Journey to the Earth's Interior, or, Have the Poles Really Been Discovered.* Aurora, Ill.: Published by the author, 1920.

Geoffrey of Monmouth, *Histories of the Kings of Britain.* Edited by Ernest Rhys. Everyman's Library, no. 577. New York: E. P. Dutton, 1975.

Graves, Tom, *Needles of Stone.* Somerset, England: Gothic Image Publications, 1986.

Group, David, *The Evidence for the Bermuda Triangle.* Wellingborough, Northampton, England: Aquarian, 1984.

Hadingham, Evan:
Circles and Standing Stones. New York: Walker, 1975.
Early Man and the Cosmos. New York: Walker, 1984.

Hargreaves, Gerald, *Atalanta: A Story of Atlantis.* London: Hutchinson & Co., 1949.

Hawkins, Gerald S., *Stonehenge Decoded.* New York: Dell, 1965.

Herbert, Glendon M., and I.S.K. Reeves, *Koreshan Unity Settlement, 1894-1977.* Orlando, Fla.: Department of Natural Resources, Division of Recreation and Parks, 1977.

Higgins, Godfrey, *The Celtic Druids.* Los Angeles: Philosophical Research Society, 1977.

Jones, Inigo, *The Most Notable Antiquity of Great Britain Vulgarly Called Stonehenge 1655.* Berkeley, Calif.: Scolar Press, 1973.

Kosok, Paul, *Life, Land and Water in Ancient Peru.* New York: Long Island University Press, 1965.

Kusche, Larry:
The Bermuda Triangle Solved. Buffalo: Prometheus, 1986.
The Disappearance of Flight 19. New York: Harper & Row, 1980.

Lytton, Edward, *The Coming Race.* Quakertown, Pa.: Philosophical Publishing Co., 1973.

McBride, James, *Symmes' Theory of Concentric Spheres Demonstrating That the Earth is Hollow, Habitable Within and Widely Open About the Poles.* Cincinnati: Morgan, Lodge, and Fisher, 1826.

Marshall, Gen. George C., "Giant Effigies of the Southwest." *National Geographic,* September 1952.

Mendelssohn, Kurt, *The Riddle of the Pyramids.* London: Thames & Hudson, 1974.

Michell, John:
The Earth Spirit: Its Ways, Shrines and Mysteries. New York: Crossroad, 1975.
The Flying Saucer Vision: The Holy Grail Restored. London: Sidgwick & Jackson, 1967.
Megalithomania. Ithaca, N.Y.: Cornell University Press, 1982.
"The Sacred Serpents of America." *The Unexplained,* no. 22. London, 1982.
Secrets of the Stone: The Story of Astroarchaeology. Harmondsworth, Middlesex, England: Penguin, 1977.
The View over Atlantis. New York: Ballantine, 1977.

Morrison, Tony:
"Aeronauts Not Astronauts," *The Unexplained,* no. 18. London, 1982.
"Enigma of the Drawings," *The Unexplained,* no. 19. London, 1982.

"Nazca: The End of the Trail," *The Unexplained,* no. 22. London, 1982.
Pathways to the Gods: The Mystery of the Andes Lines. New York: Harper and Row, 1978.

Muir, Richard:
Riddles in the British Landscape. New York: Thames and Hudson, 1981.
Traveller's History of Britain and Ireland. London: Michael Joseph Ltd., 1983.

Plato, *Timaeus and Critias.* Translated by Desmond Lee. New York: Penguin, 1971.

Poole, Lynn, and Gray Poole, *One Passion, Two Loves.* New York: Thomas Y. Crowell, 1966.

Reed, William, *The Phantom of the Poles.* New York: Walter S. Rockey and Co., 1906.

Reiche, Maria, *Mystery on the Desert.* Stuttgart, 1976.

Reinhart, Johan, *The Nazca Lines.* Lima, Peru: Editorial Los Pinos, 1985.

Reynolds, Jeremiah N., *Remarks of Symmes' Theory Which Appeared in the American Quarterly Review.* Washington, D.C.: Gales and Seaton, 1827.

Ridge, Martin, *Ignatius Donnelly: The Portrait of a Politican.* Chicago: University of Chicago Press, 1962.

Silverberg, Robert, *Moundbuilders of Ancient America.* Greenwich, Conn.: New York Graphic Society, 1968.

Smyth, Charles Piazzi, *The Great Pyramid: Its Secrets and Mysteries Revealed.* New York: Bell, 1978.

Stuart, George, "Who Were the Mound Builders?" *National Geographic,* December 1972.

Symmes, John Cleves, *Symzonia.* New York: Amo, 1975.

Teed, Cyrus Read:
Cellular Cosmogony. Philadelphia: Porcupine Press, 1975.
Fundamentals of Koreshan Universology. Estero, Fla.: Guiding Star Publishing House, 1927.

Tolstoy, Nikolai, *The Quest for Merlin.* Boston: Little, Brown and Co., 1985.

Tompkins, Peter, *Secrets of the Great Pyramid.* New York: Harper & Row, 1971.

Toth, Max, *Pyramid Prophecies.* New York: Warner, 1979.

Viola, Herman J., and Carolyn Margolis, ed., *Magnificent Voyagers: The United States Exploring Expedition, 1838-1842.* Washington, D.C.: Smithsonian Institution Press, 1985.

Von Däniken, Erich:
Chariots of the Gods? New York: G.P. Putnam's Sons, 1970.
Gods from Outer Space. New York: G.P. Putnam's Sons, 1970.

Waisbard, Simone, *The World's Last Mysteries.* Pleasantville, N.Y.: Readers Digest Association, 1978.

Woodman, Jim:
Nazca: The Flight of the Condor I. London: John Murray, 1980.
Nazca: Journey to the Sun. New York: Pocket Books, 1977.

PICTURE CREDITS

INDEX

Time-Life Books Inc.
is a wholly owned subsidiary of
TIME INCORPORATED

FOUNDER: Henry R. Luce 1898-1967

Editor-in-Chief: Henry Anatole Grunwald
Chairman and Chief Executive Officer: J. Richard Munro
President and Chief Operating Officer: N. J. Nicholas, Jr.
Chairman of the Executive Committee: Ralph P. Davidson
Corporate Editor: Ray Cave
Executive Vice President, Books: Kelso F. Sutton
Vice President, Books: George Artandi

TIME-LIFE BOOKS INC.

EDITOR: George Constable
Executive Editor: Ellen Phillips
Director of Design: Louis Klein
Director of Editorial Resources: Phyllis K. Wise
Editorial Board: Russell B. Adams, Jr., Thomas H. Flaherty,
Lee Hassig, Donia Ann Steele, Rosalind Stubenberg,
Kit van Tulleken, Henry Woodhead
Director of Photography and Research: John Conrad Weiser

PRESIDENT: Christopher T. Linen
Chief Operating Officer: John M. Fahey, Jr.
Senior Vice Presidents: James L. Mercer, Leopoldo Toralballa
Vice Presidents: Stephen L. Bair, Ralph J. Cuomo, Neal Goff,
Stephen L. Goldstein, Juanita T. James, Hallett Johnson III,
Carol Kaplan, Susan J. Maruyama, Robert H. Smith,
Paul R. Stewart, Joseph J. Ward
Director of Production Services: Robert J. Passantino

Editorial Operations
Copy Chief: Diane Ullius
Editorial Operations Manager: Caroline A. Boubin
Production: Celia Beattie
Quality Control: James J. Cox (director)
Library: Louise D. Forstall

MYSTERIES OF THE UNKNOWN

SERIES DIRECTOR: Russell B. Adams, Jr.
Series Administrator: Elise Ritter Gibson
Designer: Herbert H. Quarmby

Editorial Staff for *Mystic Places*
Associate Editors: Sara Schneidman (pictures); Pat Daniels,
Anne Horan (text)
Assistant Designer: Lorraine D. Rivard
Series Coordinator: Constance B. Strawbridge
Copy Coordinator: Carolee Belkin Walker
Picture Coordinator: Bradley Hower

Special Contributors: Christine Hinze (London, picture
researcher); Juliet Bruce, Barbara Cornell, Marie A. Fontaine,
Don Jackson, Thomas A. Lewis, J. I. Merritt, Wendy Murphy,
Dirk Olin, Jake Page, Marilynne R. Rudick, Cinda Siler, Chuck
Smith, Dan Stashower, John R. Sullivan, William Triplett,
Michael Webb (text); Henrietta Farve, Kaila Smith
(administration)

Correspondents: Elisabeth Kraemer-Singh (Bonn); Maria
Vincenza Aloisi (Paris); Ann Natanson (Rome).
Valuable assistance was also provided by Judy Aspinall
(London); Christina Lieberman (New York); Mirka Gondicas
(Athens); Traudl Lessing (Vienna); Andrea Dabrowski
(Mexico City).

The research for *Mystic Places* was prepared under the
supervision of Time-Life Books by:
Bibliographics Inc.
President: David L. Harrison
Researchers: Susan Blair, Ann Di Fiore, Isabel H. Fucigna,
Mimi Harrison, Feroline Higginson, Christian Kinney, Arna
Lane, Barbara Levitt, Patricia Paterno, Maggie Johnson
Sliker, Deborah Thornton, Diana Vanek, Elizabeth Ward
Editorial Assistant: Lona Tavernise
The Consultants:

Marcello Truzzi, professor of sociology at Eastern Michigan
University, is also director of the Center for Scientific
Anomalies Research (CSAR) and editor of its journal, the
Zetetic Scholar. Dr. Truzzi, who considers himself a "constructive skeptic" with regard to claims of the paranormal,
works through the CSAR to produce dialogues between critics and proponents of unusual scientific claims.

Tony Morrison, by profession a zoologist, is also a film mak-
er and writer. While searching for rare wildlife in South
America for more than two decades, he became fascinated
with the Andes, especially with the Nazca lines in Peru.
Among his works are *The Andes* for Time-Life Books, and
the film *Mystery of the Desert.* He is also coauthor with Gerald
Hawkins of *Pathways to the Gods.*

Peter Tompkins has spent decades researching, speculating,
and writing about sources of ancient wisdom. His book *Secrets of the Great Pyramid* is a landmark in the field. His other
works include *The Magic of Obelisks, Mysteries of the Mexican
Pyramids,* and, with Christopher Bird, *The Secret Life of Plants.*

Other Publications

TIME FRAME
FIX IT YOURSELF
FITNESS, HEALTH & NUTRITION
SUCCESSFUL PARENTING
HEALTHY HOME COOKING
UNDERSTANDING COMPUTERS
LIBRARY OF NATIONS
THE ENCHANTED WORLD
THE KODAK LIBRARY OF CREATIVE PHOTOGRAPHY
GREAT MEALS IN MINUTES
THE CIVIL WAR
PLANET EARTH
COLLECTOR'S LIBRARY OF THE CIVIL WAR
THE EPIC OF FLIGHT
THE GOOD COOK
WORLD WAR II
HOME REPAIR AND IMPROVEMENT
THE OLD WEST

*For information on and a full description of any of the Time-Life
Books series listed above, please call 1-800-621-7026,
or write:*
Reader Information
Time-Life Customer Service
P.O. Box C-32068
Richmond, Virginia 23261-2068
This volume is one of a series that examines the history and
nature of seemingly paranormal phenomena.

Library of Congress Cataloguing in Publication Data
Mystic places.
  (Mysteries of the unknown)
  Bibliography: p.
  Includes index.
  1. Archaeology — Miscellanea. 2. Occult sciences.
I. Time-Life Books.   II. Series.
BF1439.M87 1987   001.9'4   87-6540
ISBN 0-8094-6312-1
ISBN 0-8094-6313-X (lib. bdg.)